A Cavalcade of Lesser Horrors

Also by Peter Smith
Published by the University of Minnesota Press

A Porch Sofa Almanac

A CAVALCADE OF LESSER HORRORS

Peter Smith

University of Minnesota Press
Minneapolis
London

Copyright 2011 by Peter Smith

All rights reserved. No part of this publication may be reproduced, stored in a retrieval system, or transmitted, in any form or by any means, electronic, mechanical, photocopying, recording, or otherwise, without the prior written permission of the publisher.

Published by the University of Minnesota Press
111 Third Avenue South, Suite 290
Minneapolis, MN 55401-2520
http://www.upress.umn.edu

Library of Congress Cataloging-in-Publication Data
Smith, Peter, 1946–.
A cavalcade of lesser horrors / Peter Smith.
    p. cm.
ISBN 978-0-8166-7557-9 (pbk.)
1. Smith, Peter, 1946—Anecdotes. 2. Radio broadcasters—United States—Anecdotes. I. Title.
PN1991.4.S54A3 2011
791.44'0228092—dc22

                                                2011023627

Printed in the United States of America on acid-free paper

The University of Minnesota is an equal-opportunity educator and employer.

18 17 16 15 14 13 12 11   10 9 8 7 6 5 4 3 2 1

Contents

Preface

*The sins that make these essayists cringe in retrospect
usually turn out to be insensitivity that wounded another,
a lack of empathy, or the callowness of youth.*

—PHILLIP LOPATE, INTRODUCTION TO *THE ART
OF THE PERSONAL ESSAY*

I was between projects when I started to write these essays. They
were going to be exercises to keep my skills sharp while I waited
for my muse to drop something important in my lap. They were
supposed to be simple sketches, just doodles in the margins—
personal reminders about who I am, where I come from, and
what I have and have not done with my life so far. I wanted them
to be snapshots of my journey from early childhood on the South
Side of Chicago, to the suburbs, where I came of age with eight
brothers and sisters, to leaving home to come to Minnesota for
college, and from there into the army, to Vietnam, back to Minnesota, and eventually into a career in advertising.

I had hoped they would be concise, carefully drawn, well-
behaved little pieces. Sadly, no. In a few simple sentences they
took over the project rather rudely. They wrested the wheel from
my hands.

Sitting at the keyboard, watching them give birth to themselves, I was surprised at the turns these essays took, at their South

Side Irish wiseass attitude, at the subjects, settings, and themes they chose. They came at me from every possible direction.

The vast, white, post–World War II diaspora out of Chicago into the suburbs was there. So was Libertyville, the farm town turned bedroom community where we settled. There was our Catholicism, as much cultural as spiritual. The baby boom boomed, with my parents doing their part. Siblings arrived at good Catholic fifteen-month intervals, and the house became increasingly crowded and jittery. For a while, when everyone was still at home, eleven of us shared four bedrooms and a bath and a half.

Long-forgotten people, venues, and incidents returned. Back-of-the-balcony church pews where the local punks, some of them my friends, carved their initials. The drugstore soda fountain where I worked. Priests. Teachers. Doctors. Bums. The wobble-kneed high school football coach. Draft notices and Dear John letters. Long-buried embarrassments and character flaws (my own and others'). Minnesota—*ma belle* Minnesota. The false God and acid bath that is a career in advertising copywriting. And my first and only true talent—the thing I call real writing.

All of it came rushing back in extremely sharp focus. Nothing was gauzy or saccharine, and the vividness and detail incubated the theme underpinning the project: each of us lives in rich, subtle, and elegant detail to which we are, for the most part, oblivious. We see things without being aware we see them. We feel things without realizing we feel them. Subliminally sensitive to one another, we know things—often painfully personal things— about the people around us without actually knowing we know.

If these essays are honestly written—and I believe they are— then life really is, as the title says, a cavalcade of lesser horrors. Nothing so big as to scare you to death or so brutal as to cripple you for life. Just that steady drip, drip, drip of small stuff that jars you on some level, then disappears to return years later like the people, events, and small stuff recorded here.

Thank you to my wife, Mary, and our children, Samuel, Emily, Joseph, and John Henry. Thank you to my mother, my father, my brothers and sisters, and my extended family (both my wife's and my own). Thank you to Chicago, Libertyville, and Minnesota and to all the people and lesser horrors I have encountered along the way.

A Cavalcade of Lesser Horrors

South State Street

Thick green oil-based paint covered everything: streetlamps, park railings, drinking fountains, the steel girders of the Illinois Central overpass, and the wood of the Illinois Central station on 144th Street. Everything. Someone had been maintaining Chicago long before my brother and I arrived on the scene, which meant Chicago had been here long before us and was vulnerable to rust and erosion and change. Whoever had preceded us had daubed on the paint so thick that it was softening the shape of things. If Chicago wasn't rusting, then it was melting. And my brother and I, so recently arrived from wherever it was that children came from, brains growing in, were caught between the Chicago that was and the Chicago that would be on South State Street.

"Put your arm around him. Look at him," my father used to say, sitting there on the sofa, elbows on knees, smoking a cigarette. "That's the best friend you're ever going to have."

And we would. My brother and I would stand there, arms around each other's shoulders, looking at each other. The same brother who dropped the specially braced shoe the Veterans Administration had made for my father into the crib on top of me. The same brother who told me the meat grinder my mother had fixed to the kitchen table—the meat grinder she used to turn round steak into hamburger—was a merry-go-round for fingers. The same brother who pushed me into the corner of the living

1

room hassock and took a divot out of my cheek that required stitches. This was the best friend I would ever have.

Somewhere in the family photo archives is a picture of the two of us with our arms around each other, mine around his shoulders, his around my neck hugging desperately tight, all but throttling me, not simply complying with my father's directions but complying frenetically, a firstborn to the core.

And always, there was Chicago: outside the front door, up and down the block, coming in and out with aunts, uncles, cousins and grandparents. My father was a nightside police reporter in those days, and my bother and I would stand at the table and watch him roll a shift's worth of Bull Durham cigarettes to get him through a night of streetcar rides from police precinct house to precinct house to check the blotter, find out who'd been arrested, and chat up the desk sergeants. He would disappear downtown on the Illinois Central every afternoon and be back the next morning, after another night's worth of stories, smelling of sweat and fuel oil and cinnamon Life Savers and cigarettes and Juicy Fruit gum. Our world had his boundaries—his and my mother's. It stretched from their parents' houses in Blue Island and Flossmoor, north to Brookfield, east through Hazelcrest, to Hammond, Indiana, where Aunt Babe and Uncle Frank lived in an apartment over a bar (Frank working nights in a steel mill in Gary), all the way east to Chesterton, Indiana, at the south end of Lake Michigan, where my mother's mother's people still farmed.

There was a big, generous, loving family out there—a Sunday night Sealtest ice-cream cake roll of a clan that had come through the Great Depression and the war, and like every other family in every other ethnic neighborhood in the city, our family stood on the verge of postwar prosperity.

And like every other family in every other neighborhood, we were waiting for the other shoe to drop. There was an unspoken, somewhat tentative "take what you get and say nothing" sense of pleasant-but-guarded surprise when things went well. There was a "what did you expect anyhow?" resignation when they didn't.

This, then, was our first lesser horror—an unspoken sense that somehow, somewhere, something might be slipping out of kilter. My mother and father had a saying: "Everything is all right so far," they would tell each other. For a couple of Depression-era kids raising a family, it was a form of optimism, but that "so far" hung there, arching an eyebrow, admonishing, urging caution.

Reporting the news in Chicago, my father was in the business of supplying the city with cautionary tales. The *Chicago Daily News* city desk was a font of murders, mayhem, traffic accidents, theft (grand and petty), and more—incidents where everything most definitely was not all right so far. My mother had put herself through teacher's college by the time she was eighteen. It took hard work and tenacity, not sunshine and rainbows, to make sure everything stayed all right so far.

I was three years old, standing in the backyard. My older brother was there, and we were watching the garbagemen work the alley.

The crusty, flat snow was full of coal soot and dog shit. We were out there by ourselves with nothing to do, wearing heavy, hooded snowsuits, snot bubbles burbling, hoods knotted under our fat little chins. We were out there because it was naptime for brother number three, who was that good Catholic fifteen months younger than me.

Our parents were turning out to be recidivist reproducers.

"You know, dear," my grandmother had said when she explained the facts of life to my mother, "when a man and a woman marry, they have something to do with one another."

So much for birth control. They would have nine children before they broke their biological clinch and adjourned to the farthest neutral corners. Their fecundity binge, begun during Roosevelt's fourth term, ran unabated through the entirety of the

Truman and Eisenhower administrations and ended with Kennedy in the White House in March 1961. But this was not Camelot. The more children they had, the more emotionally crowded the house became. We grew up with our elbows pulled in tight to our sides.

That morning in the backyard, my older brother and I were not aware of all the siblings hurtling toward us—although standing in the backyard in the cold and the dog shit, waiting for number three to rise from his princely late-morning slumber, should have served as one hell of a good clue.

Damn number three anyhow. He was a brooding, jealous, coddled little thing. He arrived and insinuated himself between me and the parental love to which I felt so richly entitled. He usurped attention that was rightly mine. It was always "I need, I need, I need" with him. "I need strained vegetables spooned into one end. I need them removed from the diapered-and-powdered other."

Ultimately the joke would be on number three. In the house in his crib, nuzzling a warm bottle of milk in his sleep, suspirating peaceful little breaths instead of blowing frosty snot bubbles, he was unaware number four was en route. She arrived the following October. Morning naptime a year hence would find three of us banished to the dog shit–riddled backyard.

And after number four, number five. And after number five, numbers six, seven, eight, and nine. The pattern of life in the fifties had established itself.

"I have a recurring dream," my mother told me years later. She was back at work then—a high school librarian.

"I am pregnant, and so...very..." She searched for precisely the right word the way librarians do. "Disappointed."

She will turn ninety soon, and there is a part of me that wouldn't be the least bit surprised if she showed up for her birthday party wearing fifties-style maternity garb and telling us, "You have a new brother or sister on the way."

At any rate, there we were, my older brother and me, cheeks chapping and snot smearing, watching the garbagemen work the alley.

They had passed our house, and were three doors down the alley, heading north toward 143rd, when one of them came skulking back to our house. He reached over the fence and took my tricycle. He slung it over his back, and looking over his shoulder at us, he carried it off like a Mother Goose fox carrying away a sack full of chickens.

He walked up to the driver's side of the truck and pounded on the door with the flat of his hand. The driver opened the door, and the thief handed my tricycle up to him. Then the thief climbed onto that little platform beside the hopper at the back of the truck and took one more look back at us as the truck rolled away.

A lesser horror took hold—one with watery blue eyes and a cruel, eastern European cabbage-soup face. I don't think I would have been able to tell my mother what had happened. I don't think I had the experience or the vocabulary yet. Even if I had, those eyes and that face would have stopped me. Everything was not all right so far, but I'd be damned if I'd say so.

Sometimes, I think he took the tricycle home to his own son. Sometimes I think he sold it for scrap. He would be almost ninety now, so lately I've taken to thinking of him as a cruel-looking old corpse, rosary knotted in his vodka-fat fingers, mourned and lovingly remembered by his middle-aged son. After all, didn't he bring him a tricycle?

The snow melted. Summer came. Life proceeded. One afternoon, my brother and I found a can of Chicago green enamel, and sitting number three on the curb, we proceeded to give him a rich, thick coat of paint.

A Teaspoon of Water

In some other life, when I am some other writer, I am going to have to come to terms with water: to cope with it as a metaphor, to make it flow where and how I want it to flow, sometimes seeming to pour down stairs the way the Gallatin River does in the mountains above Bozeman, Montana, or sometimes barely moving, brooding and moody like a Mississippi River backwater below Winona, Minnesota. In some other life, I am going to have to come to terms with water once and for all. It's too simple and complex for me now.

We were at Aunt Blanche's house in Hazelcrest—Aunt Blanche, my father's sister, über-Catholic and mother of a multitude of slightly older cousins. My mother's mother had died and we, the three oldest, boys ages eight, six, and four, were spending the night at Aunt Blanche's while my mother, her father, and her sisters worked out the details that amost immediately overrun death. My father had hurried us over after supper. We'd arrived in the dark, clumped into the kitchen with all our stuff in that cheap old suitcase that only came out for overnight visits like this, and now here we were, left in her custody.

She was older than my father, and the relationship between them—indeed, the relationship between all seven of his siblings—had long since set up firm. It was close and yet not close. It takes quite a while to have seven children, and my grandparents had strewn theirs across a decade and a half. Blanche had

6

been one of the older ones, while my father had come along later, and in looking back, she seems to have been part big sister, part mother to him and his two younger brothers.

Now, home from the war, married and settled down, the younger brothers were family men with young children. Her children were older. The bond between Blanche and my father had loosened, except for occasions like this.

Damn, she was Catholic—the most austere Catholic in an austerely Catholic family. When my father's brother Dan married a Baptist girl and the two of them produced a child, Blanche and Aunt Maggie dropped by unannounced one Sunday morning and offered to babysit while the young couple went to church. The parents were barely out of sight before my aunts baptized the boy Catholic in the kitchen sink.

It was her nature. Her soul longed and thirsted for the Lord. She wanted, among other things, to be a fruitful vine and give her children to Him. Already, one of her daughters had entered the convent, and if none of her sons developed a vocation for the priesthood, it wasn't for Blanche's lack of trying. I am sure she offered them to Him on her knees beside her bed every night.

So my father's half-mother, half-sister was our slightly stern half-grandmother, half-aunt. She wore nunlike shoes and longer dresses, and her face was beginning to take on a certain sallow sag that came down my grandmother's side of the family—a sag that, standing in the bathroom, rinsing my razor as I shave, I recognize in the mirror now. Back then it scared the hell out of me.

To be in her presence was to be stuck in the late thirties and to have to be on your toes. You never knew when she might hurl a Baltimore Catechism question your way—and not a question from the first few pages that you'd memorized in that first fit of academic fervor last fall. A question from deeper in the book and the school year, when you had decided you were not going to put in the effort to become a theological whiz kid. She gave you the same Holy Roller willies that nuns did. You weren't sure what she was all about, but you were sure it was spiritual and that you, being young, male, and Chicago Irish on your mother's side, were predestined to lead a more secular life—a Studs Lonigan life—from which Aunt Blanche was out to save you.

Uncle Bob spooked around the edges of all this, a graying, also sallow presence in shirtsleeves and necktie, hands in pockets, jingling his change. He was round-shouldered, a middle-class accountant/prince consort to her would-be virgin mother.

Near the end of his life, my father told me about an evening when he and his brothers found Blanche and Bob, courting then, horizontal on the living room couch. The thrill was long gone by the time my brothers and I arrived to spend the night.

Acerbic, maybe a little dyspeptic, Uncle Bob lurked in the background. One or two of our older cousins must have been around the house somewhere, too, but the big old place felt dark, quiet, substantial, and empty to us—like a funeral home. Light pooled under end table lamps in the living room. The air was overheated and still. Like Aunt Blanche herself, the place seemed stuck in a Catholic 1938, with small holy water fonts beneath the light switches and crucifixes and holy cards and holy pictures everywhere. A picture of Jesus pointing to heaven with one hand and to his Sacred Heart with the other hung on the wall outside the bathroom. His heart, and I can only assume Aunt Blanche's, were on fire.

She had all three of us in the bathtub. She was on her knees washing us instead of on her knees praying, when the phone rang. She used the edge of the tub to push herself up, and as she left the room, she looked back and raised a warning finger like Jesus pointing to heaven.

"Don't move," she said somewhat sternly. "You know, you can drown in a single teaspoonful of water."

I was at once horrified. This was stunning information. I was not surprised that word of this vulnerability would come at us from Aunt Blanche. She was, after all, a religious person with bad news to impart, and religious people always seemed to enjoy imparting bad news—or proscriptions or interdictions or admonitions. Anything with "Thou shalt not." Even then I knew religious people loved killing joy. If they could, they would drown it in a teaspoonful of water.

The soul of our so recently departed grandmother seemed to circle overhead, a guardian angel now, protecting my brothers and me from the thousands of teaspoonfuls of water in which we were sitting, not moving a muscle. For all I knew, at that very moment, there were dead people at kitchen tables in apartments all over the city, pitched forward, facedown in teaspoons full of water even as elevated trains full of tired men and women on their way home from work rattled by.

Only the summer before, my older brother and I had begun swimming lessons at the local pool. Nowhere in any of our instructions had the teacher said anything about drowning in teaspoons. I was fairly certain Aunt Blanche had immersed us deeply into hyperbole, that she had baptized us yet again with water and overadmonishment. I wasn't positive, but I was pretty sure. Up to my bellybutton in water, I wasn't going to move. Neither were my brothers. This and Jesus' love are the only reasons we were still alive when Aunt Blanche got back.

She got us out of the tub, dried us, and put us into our pajamas, after which we adjourned to the living room to kneel in a row along the sofa and say a decade of the rosary for poor dead Grandma.

Minutes later all three of us were in one bed with the lights out and the bedroom door cracked open a sliver. Down the hall, past the picture of Jesus and his Sacred Heart, a leaky bathroom faucet plinked every so often, reminding me that in some other life, when I am some other writer, I am going to have to come to terms with water.

Pop's Wound

It was late on a summer evening on the way home from Aunt Maggie and Uncle Jack's. I was standing in the back of the car, leaning over the front seat, my older brother riding shotgun. My father was telling us again about the day he was wounded in the war.

His outfit was making another landing on another South Pacific beach. A Japanese machine gun had them pinned down, and he and another GI were crawling up an embankment to attack the position when an American mortar round fell short. A piece of shrapnel nicked a nerve high in his leg, and the leg never worked right again.

His ankle flopped, and he was constantly spraining it in spite of the specially braced shoes the Veterans Administration made for him. The damaged nerve sent false messages—messages about cramps and spasms and stabs of pain. The meat was gone, and where the shrapnel had gone in there was a deep dimple instead. At the bottom of the dimple, under the scar, that piece of shrapnel remained pinned up against the nerve. The army doctors had decided not to risk removing it.

"Want to feel it?" he asked us that night in the car. "Go ahead. Stick your finger in. Feel it."

I remember the moon coming up big and yellow; the tone and cadence of the White Sox play-by-play man's voice on the car radio; my father in his early thirties that night, riding the happy and charming upside of his sine wave. Maybe it was one of those rare days when nothing hurt.

I remember my own wave—one of complete revulsion. He was old. So was the wound. Who knew what I might find down there at the bottom of that hole?

My brother didn't feel any such qualms. "Okay," he said, and my father guided my brother's index finger to a point between his right pocket and the seam down the leg of his pants.

"There. Feel it?"

"Yeah. Wow."

I was not surprised that my brother had accepted the invitation so eagerly and so cheerfully. He had absolute faith in my father. I did not, not even then.

"Not me, Pop. No thanks." My father's war had taken place long before I'd shown up. His experience, his wound, his occasional bouts of malaria—all that stuff belonged with his dog tags and Purple Heart in his handkerchief drawer, where a kid could sneak a look at it now and then and parse his own picture of what the old man had gone through and what it all had meant. I wasn't about to stick my finger in there. It didn't belong. His war and his wound were his business.

I've often thought that the men who fought in the jungles of New Guinea must have come to look on whatever life they had after 1944 as bonus time. Much later, when he was an old man and retired to northern Wisconsin, my father put his finger on a map and said, "This is where we were in combat for eighty-nine straight days." He told me that he'd become delirious with dengue fever, crawled into a cave, passed out, and came to three days later to find his buddies still fighting. He'd picked up his rifle and gone back to work. He told me once that the second time his unit was sent from Australia up to New Guinea, every man on the ship expected to be killed.

Then he got wounded, and for all the pain and the crippling, it was a million-dollar wound. It saved his life and got him back to Chicago where, a week after he arrived, he married the most beautiful girl on the South Side and entered bonus time. Eleven months later, my brother arrived. Fifteen months after that, I showed up. And so on and so forth until the home in the suburbs—the one he'd made with the most beautiful girl on the South Side—was full of healthy, bright children.

He must have been living the bonus time enigma again that night. The White Sox on the radio...two sons in the car...and somewhere in his subconscious what had happened in New Guinea, all of it coming out in the telling of the story again, coming out not so much for my brother's and my benefit as to help him sift through it all once more.

The hole in his leg was a door. On this side, Ike was in the White House. The economy was booming. Life was good. On the other side, it was always 1943. No thanks, Pop. I'll pass.

A year after he died, I had a dream. I was one of three men in the New Guinea jungle, and we ambushed a Japanese patrol that was set up to ambush Americans. It was the most vivid dream I have ever had, right down to the sound of blood hissing from a throat I had slit and the smell of the feces oozing from a bayonet wound in a dead man's belly. I can still feel the horror of watching blood flow across the narrow muddy path and worrying some Japanese soldier might see it and sound the alarm.

It was a practical and dirty little dream about a practical and dirty little piece of war business, and I do not doubt that Pop sent it to me—writer to writer. He took me by the wrist and stuck my finger into the hole. I know it was him because at the end of the dream, when all the Japanese were dead and we were standing there, looking at what we had done, it began to snow the kind of thin early winter snow that I'd seen fall on his grave in Libertyville. I could almost hear the semi tires singing on the Tri-State Tollway.

A Crisis of Faith

Roman Catholicism as we grew up in it was a peasant's faith; an urban, industrialized extension of the agrarian religion practiced by generations and centuries of blunt, brooding serfs scattered over the landscape from Ireland to Poland, from Portugal to the Balkans, where it came up against Greek Orthodoxy and Islam, where it—well, balkanized. There was a church every five miles across the old country, whatever old country you happened to be from, and a priest in every church—the representative of a bishop, who was a representative of a cardinal, who was a representative of the pope—one holy and apostolic spiritual Ponzi scheme. Kneel anywhere on the continent of Europe today and you can feel them—eleven hundred pre-Reformation years' worth of dearly departed Catholic peasants and their priests, asleep in the Lord, waiting for Judgment Day. And five hundred more years of that volatile mixture of true Catholic believers and the benighted skeptics whom Luther and others lured away.

Catholic churches weren't five miles apart in Chicago. They were closer. There was one or more steeples protruding like pins from a huge map in a hundred ethnic communities— Slavs, Czechs, Slovenians, Italians, Poles, Irish. Neighborhoods were full of families three or fewer generations removed from some agrarian hovel—meat-handed, factory-working families with mute, hard-eyed grandmothers clutching rosaries and coin purses and peering out from under babushkas and equally mute

13

grandfathers and great-uncles, lost and broken, eyes looking back to a homeland that never really was, at least not like they remembered it.

All the Catholic churches and holy fervor in the world couldn't seem to save Chicago from polio in the summer back then. The city would be so hot and so humid that you could smell the concrete sweat under last winter's coal soot, and still they would have to shut down the swimming pools and the drinking fountains. Polio. Infantile paralysis. The disease was a parent's nightmare. One day your child was fine, the next day he or she was in bed with a fever. The doctor came around, made his diagnosis, and the whole family began a watch to see how far the disease would advance. When polio killed the tough kid across the street, the kid who routinely beat up my brothers and me, my parents sold the house and headed for the fresh, healthy air of Libertyville, a northern suburb of the city, where Saint Joseph's Catholic school and church and the Sisters of Mercy were waiting.

Saint Joseph's was a moderately large, dark, older church with a main aisle and two side aisles and walls of stained glass windows. There was a smallish foyer where one of the ushers would sit at a card table and count the collection money from the last mass as you walked in. A creaky set of stairs twisted up to the balcony. The church organ was up there and a gray milquetoast organist fiddling with the stops, trying to avoid eye contact with the young local tough guys—guys whose peasant-devout mothers made them get up and go to mass, guys with ducktail haircuts in a style we called a "Chicago boxcar," cut short and flat on top and swept back into a ducktail on the sides. *Très* chic and *très* tough.

You couldn't see the altar from the back pews up there. Except for one rumple-suited, flat-footed usher making the collection, you were pretty much unsupervised. Generations of hard guys had brooded away years of homilies, carving their initials and those of their girlfriends into the ever-darkening wood of the pews. The pews read like a who's who of Libertyville sinners.

You didn't start out up in the balcony. It took years to get there. Your parents held you in their arms downstairs at first, then you stood on the kneeler beside them while they held your younger siblings. Eventually, you were indentured to the Sisters of Mercy—a sorority of second- and third-generation immigrant daughters who had opted for the veil instead of the babushka. The sisters issued a paperback copy of the Baltimore Catechism to you, which you folded in half and carried in the back pocket of your corduroy school pants.

First Holy Communion followed, then a tour of duty as an altar boy and confirmation. If you weren't priest material (and sent to the diocese preparatory seminary), you went to public high school and continued your spiritual growth at the parochial school after supper on Wednesday evenings. It was boys in one classroom, girls in another, with just enough time to hang out on the steps and grab a quick juvenile delinquent cigarette before class began. This was the natural order of things. Only when you were through with high school, only when you had dropped out and gone to work or graduated, could you ascend those creaky, twisting balcony stairs and take your place among the dark, young male peasant faithful in those back pews.

There were crises of faith along the way, any number of them. The Sisters of Mercy had long since established a hierarchy of religious hyperbole. Following a tradition that disappears into the depths of the Dark Ages, they dramatized, romanticized, and embellished Catholic theology quite a bit. Their overstatements ranged out and fell along and either side of a line that demarcated the boundary between dogma and bunk.

You were torn. Part of you—the part where you were (and always would be) your Catholic mother's son—wanted to be a good little serf and believe. Part of you—the part that wanted to ascend to the back of the balcony—wanted to defer belief, to just think about whatever the nuns had told you for a while.

The nun's bunk was, I think, especially hard on firstborn children in larger Catholic families. They had that unique relationship with parents and, by extension, with other adults. They had to be good and to swallow a little more of whatever the nuns were feeding us whole, to accept it, quite literally, on faith. Those of us who came along later could hang in the shadows, observe, and, perhaps with a little lowbrow peasant cunning, avoid whatever it was the older kids had to believe.

When Sister told us to pray for Pope Pius XII because he'd had hiccups for months, I was skeptical. I was skeptical, too, when she explained we could pare hundreds of years off our time in purgatory by repeating the prayers on the back of a holy card over and over again.

My older brother, on the other hand, was a true believer. One night at Aunt Maggie's, he told her he wanted to be the first American pope when he grew up. In pursuit of this post, he took the nuns at their word, and at night after the lights were out, engaged in discussion—more of a soliloquy, actually—concerning the deeper theological issues of childhood. Any attempt to flag him off the looming collision with reason fell on deaf ears.

And so it was that, in preparing him to receive First Holy Communion, Sister Whoever-It-Was-At-The-Time told him his rosary was more powerful than the atomic bomb. This was no doubt a variation on an ancient nun-peasant theme that predated the atomic bomb and the rosary. It seemed to me that nuns must have always told children that prayer was more powerful than the most formidable weapon of the day: more powerful than the gun, the bow, the sword, the spear, the cudgel, the sling, the stick, the rock.

It seemed, too, that it might not be prudent to repeat Sister's claim in the presence of non-Catholics. A little hyperbole just among us might not hurt, but you didn't need that kind of talk getting around.

But my brother believed. He believed with the fervor that had made our Irish ancestors so vulnerable to the faith when

Saint Patrick came evangelizing. Not content to simply believe, he felt called to go forth and evangelize too. He would be the voice of one crying in the Libertyville wilderness, starting with the Lutheran pagan kid living across the street.

"See this?" he asked the kid one morning at the school bus stop. He opened his cupped hands and showed him his rosary. "It's more powerful than the atomic bomb."

The kid took a look.

"Bullshit," he said. He may have been pagan, but he had a meticulously scientific Scandinavian mind. He proceeded to present a compelling case for the power of the atomic bomb. It was science and logic versus faith, and I would be willing to bet that, even then, the pagan kid knew more about science than Sister did. He did Luther and Niels Bohr proud.

I was willing to split the difference, but not my brother. There was absolute scorn in his eyes as he listened, a sneering "oh ye of little faith" disdain. There was a bit of back-and-forth, but in short order, the two of them were at an impasse.

So my brother threw his rosary into the weeds across the street—threw it like Audie Murphy threw hand grenades in the movies. Then he dropped to his knees and plugged his ears with his fingers and waited for Armageddon. I remember that instant of absolute terror as it arced across the spring morning sky and dropped toward the ground with horrible inevitability.

Nothing...

Nothing...

Either the nun had been lying or my brother had been issued a dud rosary. Whatever the case, my brother was rattled. His faith was shaken to its core. By kid standards, the pagan was gracious in victory. He sneered, but just a little.

"The bus is coming," he said.

I remember kicking through the weeds, helping my brother look for his dud rosary, feeling the sense of betrayal radiating off him. I was witnessing the birth of an agnostic. He would endure all the rites and undergo the usual sacraments, but he would never completely believe the nuns—or Holy Mother the Church—again. The older he got, the more betrayed and bitter he became.

My schism was softer and infinitely less angry. I just let my faith slip away like my confirmation scapular. I had worn it day and night like spiritual dog tags until it had finally rotted and fallen off while we were swimming in Lake Michigan. I stood in four feet of water and watched it drift away and sink. I could have reached out and rescued it, but I just let it go.

Soon after, Saint Joseph's launched a building drive and built a new church—a round one with superb lines of sight and no balcony. They tore down the old church. I think it's a parking lot now. Most of the nuns are asleep in the Lord now. Kneel anywhere in the Archdiocese of Chicago and you can feel them there, waiting in patient, peasant expectation for Judgment Day.

I will spare my brother the euphemisms. He died. He died an atheist. That was it. The show was over. The end. I remain here for the time being, my agnosticism a little softer and less certain than his atheism. Who knows? Who can say?

Maybe, when I die, I'll find myself in the foyer of old Saint Joe's. I'll go up those creaky stairs to the balcony, and there he'll be—using the metal-framed corner of his rosary crucifix to carve his initials into that last pew.

The Denunciation

I ratted Steve Geary out to Sister Clotilde after First Holy Communion. I denounced him, as vilely, as weakly, and as abjectly as any human ever exposed another. I have felt terrible about it ever since.

Sister was a sharp-faced, sharp-tongued, quick and feisty little woman with a nasty streak from a large Irish family. I wouldn't have been surprised to learn that some or all of her brothers had fought professionally as welterweights in that era when the Irish still produced great boxers. For that matter, I wouldn't have been surprised if Sister herself had been a Catholic Youth Organization flyweight champion before entering the convent. She carried herself with a certain spiritual swagger. Neither Sister nor Jesus was there to take any guff from us.

She reigned over a classroom on the first floor of the old school. The windows were high in the wall, where they could let in light without allowing us to see outside. There were the usual tall old cabinets and bookshelves and tall old radiators, too, superheated and hissing radiators covered with decades of multicolored drips from melted crayons. There was a picture of the pope and a statue of the Virgin standing atop the world, crushing the devil in the form of a snake under her foot. Two afternoons a week from mid-March to May, Sister would reach up under her coif, extract a small watch from some hidden pocket, and announce it was time to turn our attention to First Holy Communion.

19

There was much to learn. There was the matter of understanding sin—original, venial, and mortal—and all the ways to commit sin. There was the sacrament of confession and new prayers and new rites to commit to memory.

Mostly, though, there was one thing that Sister had to drill into our curly-haired little heads: Do not touch the communion host after Father puts it on your tongue. Don't touch it. Don't chew it, either. Just open your mouth, stick out your tongue, and after he puts it there, swallow it whole. Ga-lumph.

This was not her first rodeo. She knew there would be laggards among us. No matter how hard she preached, someone would find the taste strange or get the host stuck to the roof of his mouth. If she saw anyone touch the host, there would be consequences. If you saw anyone touch the host, you were to tell her.

It would taste like bread, check. Don't touch, check. No sticking it to the roofs of our mouths, check, check, check. Tell Sister if anyone touches the host, check.

The big day finally came—a Saturday in May, with the lilacs in bloom in the garden between the church and the rectory where the parish priests walked and read their breviaries. Boys wore blue pants, white shirts, and special-issue blue neckties. Girls wore white First Communion dresses. We stood on the school stairs, row upon baby boom row, while the town photographer ducked in and out from under the dark cloth at the back of his glass-plate camera.

"You—a little to the left...yeah. You—slick that hair down."

He took the picture. Organ music began flowing out of the church, and we formed up in lines just like we'd rehearsed. We marched in, boys to the right, girls to the left, Sister's last words to us echoing in our well-washed little ears: "Now remember, no touching the host."

They still said mass in Latin in those days, and it was hard to behave and pay attention even if this was our First Holy Communion. May is Mary's month, and people had decorated the area around the statue of the Virgin with lilac blooms. The place smelled of lilacs and candles and sweeping compound.

The big moment arrived, and we went forward to kneel at the communion rail and receive. Steve Geary was to my left. Father and the altar boy came from our right, and suddenly it was my turn. I opened wide, stuck out my tongue, and boom. There it was on my tongue. Communion.

The taste was unlike any bread I'd known. Not like Wonder bread, that was for damned sure. It was vaguely cardboardish—wheaty cardboard, perhaps—and the texture was that of coagulated library paste. And when I tried to swallow it, the wafer actually did stick to the roof of my mouth. In a panic, I worked it free with my tongue, swallowed it, and turned to see how Steve was doing.

He turned to me, in slow motion, with a look of absolute revulsion on his face. Evidently the taste of the Body of Christ didn't agree with him. He opened his mouth, reached in, took the host out, and holding it between thumb and forefinger, gave me a look of complete disgust. Yuk. Then he put it back in and struggled to yag it down, and we returned to our pew.

Mass didn't last long after that. There was only the matter of cleaning things up and blessing us all. I spent the time struggling with my conscience. Should I tell Sister? Should I not tell Sister? On one hand, she had told us to be on the lookout and to report host touchers. On the other hand, there was the kid code of honor. You didn't turn in another kid to an adult, and you damned sure didn't turn in a kid to a nun. This was serious stuff. This was a thorny issue. We were talking about the body of Christ here. Sure, it tasted like strep throat. Sure, it stuck to the roof of your mouth like peanut butter. But it was the body of Christ. What to do...

I told. God help me, I told. I told, and I've carried the stain ever since. I don't know what Sister did to Steve Geary, but I know what I did to myself that day. I subordinated my conscience to authority. It was the first time. It would not be the last. Such a sad, weak, malleable little man. Such a sad, weak, malleable little soul.

I am sorry, Steve Geary, wherever you are.

Absolution

If the nuns in parochial school were right all those years ago, then one of these days my soul will depart this cellulite-riddled temple and return to heaven where its maker, Almighty God, will sit in judgment. As I envision it, He will get up and walk around, sizing my soul up and looking it over as if He were the man behind the counter at an equipment rental place and my soul were a power washer I was returning.

I'll stand there, hands in my pockets, trying to look innocent. God will rub at a scratch here, rattle a lever there, and make a few notes.

"Any problems?" he'll ask casually but ominously.

"Nah," I'll lie. "Everything was cool."

The nuns told me my soul was lily-white when I arrived. Now, though, it's as stained as the pocket t-shirt on the guy at the bait shop—the one who dips snuff. And every stain comes with a story in which I succumb to another moral weakness or fall in with bad companions or pass up an opportunity to do good. It's always something I did. Or something I didn't do. If my soul really were a t-shirt, it would be tie-dyed in the lurid colors of the seven deadly sins.

The nuns told me my soul was a kind of holy chit board for keeping score in my lifelong war with temptation. The way they explained it, if I kept my soul clean, I would go right to heaven when I died. If I scuffed it up a little, I would go to purgatory and

23

endure thousands of years of cleansing fire before the purgatory parole board released me into heaven's general population. If my soul were stained with mortal sin, I would go straight to hell.

They gave me holy cards with pictures of saints on one side and prayers on the other. They said that every time I said the prayers I would reduce my sentence to purgatory by thousands of years. I slept in a bottom bunk in a room with two brothers in those days, and I kept those cards tucked under the slats that held the upper bunk overhead: the Sacred Heart, the Virgin Mother, Saint Francis, Saint Joseph, the Archangel Michael. I would lie there and say the prayers over and over again with the rote, rhythmic tedium of the Ladies' Rosary Guild under the direction of old Father Lowry, rapping out decades over a corpse at McMurrough's funeral home. Some nights, I would get in a zone, and praying under my breath, I would knock hundreds of thousands of years off my sentence for sins I hadn't committed yet.

As hard as I prayed, sin always seemed to have the upper hand. There were so many to commit, and it was all so easy, especially from the nuns' point of view. As best I could tell, they held all children in low esteem, but boys were the lowest of the low. They were the daughters of immigrant peasant families— Irish and Polish, Czech and Italian—and they had grown up with brothers who must have tormented them terribly. They taught with chips on their shoulders. Woe unto the boy child whose index finger strayed up a nostril or who, hoping to remain continent until the lavatory break before recess, crimped himself off while standing in line waiting for a word to come his way in the class spelling contest. Justice came hurtling out of nowhere in the form of a slap to the back of the head or a knuckle rap to the soft spot on top.

"Ow! Jesus, sister!" said one boy in the third grade when knuckled on the soft spot. Sister knuckled his soft spot again. "Jesus!" Sister did it again. "Jesus!" She did it again. Their comedic timing was vaudevillian and impeccable.

Sin was everywhere. If a boy was going to keep his soul even a dingy, Brand X shade of gray, he had to go to confession late on Saturday afternoon—*every* Saturday afternoon *without fail*.

So every Saturday afternoon without fail, my brothers and I appropriated the family bicycle fleet and pedaled through town to church. It was a short, quick trip, with the three of us pushing along tree-lined streets as fast as we could. Quick was the whole idea for Saturday confession: in quick, through quick, and out quick. We would come shooting across the playground in front of the school and church, up to the steps of the church itself, braking, dismounting, and letting our bikes go. We'd be three steps up the stairs before our bikes rolled to a stop and fell inert on the walk.

Flush with energy from the ride, we would burst into the back of the somber old building. Like a gang of outlaws entering a saloon, we'd bang the doors open. Old women with babushkas on their heads would turn and scowl toothless scowls in the perpetual twilight. People waiting in line outside the confessionals would look up. Other kids would smirk in recognition. Then we would remember where we were, and hitting the holy water font, crossing ourselves, sliding into the first available pew, and dropping to our knees, we would settle into the spirit of the sacrament.

They never turned on the lights for afternoon confession. The enormous room was always dark, and noises—the clank of coins in the vigil candle rack or the clack of the janitor's push broom as he swept—echoed. Below the echoes, serving as a baffle, were the murmurs of penitents and confessors—the low, steady exchange of sins and penance and prayers.

It was all very sobering. An hour ago we had been goofing off with the guys. Five minutes ago, we'd been riding our bikes as fast as we could. Now we were here in the enormous, silent dark. It was almost enough to slow us up and make us really contemplate existence. Almost, but not quite. We had a mission to accomplish. We had to get in, get our souls scrubbed, and get out. Fast.

The nuns called the first phase of confession examining one's conscience. You knelt there, mentally drumming your fingers and inventorying all your sins and transgressions. You conducted a kind of "hmmm, let's see" rumination, looking in every corner of your soul for every possible form of ruination.

The nuns' assumption—a flawed one as far as I was concerned—was that nine-year-old boys had consciences to examine. I certainly did not. There was a lingering innocence. I lacked the guile and experience to sin seriously and consistently, although guile was beginning to take root. Once established, it would prove impossible to grub out. My willful and profligate sinning continues to evolve and expand to this very day. Trust me, I know. I know because I perpetually examine my conscience. I go over everything with a fine-tooth comb. I have sinned. Boy howdy, have I sinned.

Back then, though, any sins I might have committed were crude, grubby little things, not the work of the artisan of sin I have become. What's more, the ground rules were vague. Where did routine kid bunko leave off and real lying begin? Would blaming my brother for drinking the last of the milk when I did it result in time in purgatory? And what about sex? One time, when a neighbor lady was showing us a dime-store turtle in a pan full of water on the ground, I accidentally saw down the front of her blouse. I looked away, and asked God to forgive me. Then I looked again. Deliberately. The nuns were right. I was just one more dirty, sinful boy. In bed that night, I pulled the holy card of the Sacred Heart out from under the bed slat overhead and prayed sixty thousand years off my purgatory time. Sixty thousand years seemed about right for two breasts and for coveting my neighbor's wife.

The more deeply you examined your conscience, the more thorny the enigmas you encountered. Thorniest of all was the riddle you created when you confessed to sins you did not commit.

This happened quite a bit. There were two ways you could

wander into this conundrum. You could find yourself without sin, yet having to come up with something to confess to the priest. The best thing to do in that situation was to make up a lie about having lied to your mother or father. Not once, but a specific number of times. I always said three. Lying three times to one's parents over the course of one week seemed plausible. And since you hadn't actually lied to them at all, whatever penance the priest might assign (say five Our Fathers and five Hail Marys) should more than cover the real sin (lying about lying during confession).

Or you might decide to make up and confess a sin in lieu of a sin you really had committed—a sin that was just too big to confess. Coveting your neighbor's wife as I had, for example. I couldn't tell the priest I'd peeked down the neighbor lady's blouse. No boy in his right mind could do that. So I would substitute another, more childlike sin. Stealing a candy bar was always good. It was worse than lying to a parent, but not as bad as looking down a blouse when you were supposed to be looking at a dime-store turtle. To balance things out—to establish an equivalency between candy bar theft and blouse peeking—I copped to repeat offenses and confessed to stealing seven candy bars—one at a time. It seemed about right.

The idea was to get in, get absolved, and get out fast. So you examined your conscience and cobbled together your list of sins, real and imagined, as fast as you could, then looked for the shortest line at the confessionals.

There were two traditional confessionals at the back of the church. They had doors and gave you a little privacy, and when things were busy, the lines for these confessionals were long. Penitents stood patiently, waiting their turns, trying not to overhear what the priests and the penitents kneeling in the confessionals were discussing.

In and out fast. You tried to pick the line that would move quickest. You could tell by looking at the people in line. A line full of kids, teens, and young men tended to move fast. They had made their various deals with the devil and were happy to mill themselves past the priest and go. Lines with slightly more devout adults—people with rosaries knotted in their knuckles or people who appeared to be struggling with moral issues—always bogged down a bit. These were people whose souls were works in progress. They were lumps of coal en route to becoming diamonds.

Worst of all was any confessional line with an old woman in it. They had much more finely tuned senses of sin and tended to go on and on once the little door in the confessional slid open and the priest's ear was there. Kneeling in the dark, waiting my turn, I once overheard a nearly deaf old woman confess she'd been angry when someone slammed a door and her soufflé fell.

"I said, 'God damn it,' Father," she said, unaware we could all hear. "It was only a soufflé, and there I was, asking Almighty God to damn it for falling. Or was I asking God to damn the situation?"

Meanwhile, in line outside the confessional, time was wasting. There were only so many Saturday afternoons in a childhood, God damn it.

If the lines at both confessionals were long, you had another, slightly less palatable option. Two-thirds of the way up the center aisle of the church, old Father Lowry, half deaf, sat on a folding chair facing the altar, reading his breviary, a screen of some sort next to him, and a kneeler on the other side of the screen. It was a confessional without walls. Between his hearing problem and the fact that your confession played out in front of everyone in the church, there was hardly ever a line for Father Lowry. He was a Type A clergyman. I once saw him say an entire weekday low mass in Latin in eight and a half minutes. He heard confessions with a "cut to the chase, boy—what did you do?" pragmatism. It would have been perfect except for his hearing problem.

You'd be going along in a whisper. He would hold up a hand and stop you dead. "Go back and start over. Speak up. Couldn't hear a darned word."

You'd go back and start over, and he would cup a hand to his ear and lean toward you. If that weren't enough, he would turn his hand over and gesture—louder. On one of Father's bad days, you might wind up shouting your sins to the entire church.

He brought a certain gruff, old man's incredulity to the job, too. "You did what?" he would ask in a voice loud enough to make a soufflé fall. "How many times?"

He'd heard more than fifty years of confessions by then, but to me, all those sins—hundreds of thousands of them—had been minor transgressions. What had those sinners known about looking down blouses? I was afraid if I told the old priest the truth, I would trigger a spate of high-volume righteous indignation right out there in front of God and everyone. I imagined him standing up, knocking the screen aside, and, one index finger holding his place in his breviary, pointing toward the door with the other, casting me out of the church forever.

So I confessed I stole candy bars. Seven times. And kneeling there, I stole a glimpse at the back of the church where my brothers and the guys waited in the regular confessional lines, smirking. And the old women in babushkas scowled. And I repeated the charges and specifications I'd trumped up against myself again when Father told me to speak up. He gave me my penance and absolved me of sins I had not committed. And I walked back up the aisle, knelt, said my penance as fast as I could, then genuflected and dodged out of the church to wait for my brothers and the frantic Hell's Angels bike ride home.

I have perfected sinning since then. It's all right here on my eternal soul.

Time marches on. I imagine a lot of familiar faces in the crowd as I walk up to God's throne on Judgment Day. Father Lowry and the nuns will be on hand, of course. And the lady with her goddamned soufflé, both of them risen again, hallelujah.

I shall carry my poor, frayed soul back to the Lord like a banner before me, hanging from a stick from a ragged Des Plaines river-bottom box elder. Or maybe I'll bring it stiff and flat on a shovel—like a road-killed skunk no one wants to touch—or perhaps chewed all to hell like a library book the puppy got to. You know what I'm saying—the worse for wear.

No "well done, thou good and faithful servant" for me. But maybe, if I play my holy cards right, purgatory won't be that bad in the long run.

Mortality

I was eleven years old and watching a Saturday matinee at the Liberty Theater when I realized I would die someday. Every kid in town was there. Every kid in town went to the movies every week back then. Every Saturday you played outside in the morning, came home, ate lunch, got a quarter from your mother, and raced to the movies as fast as you could.

The man who owned the theater was about sixty, and every week, before the movie began, he slumped down the aisle wearing the same baggy gray suit—your grandfather's suit—like the one Broderick Crawford wore on *Highway Patrol* on television. He would trudge up the stairs on those flat feet of his, slump out to center stage, and hold his hands out in front of himself to quiet us down—like Al Jolson quieting a vaudeville crowd. Then he would launch into the same tired speech: "Saturday matinees aren't a right, gang. We don't have to put on your kind of shows, and if you don't behave, we'll stop showing the kind of movies you like."

Feigning chastisement, we would give him his moment of silence, but he knew it was futile. We knew it was futile. The ushers and the ladies at the candy counter knew it was futile. Saturday matinees may not have been a right, but all those quarters sure as hell counted up. Every seat in the house was taken. The whole town knew all hell was about to break loose, but what could he do? What could anyone do?

Sighing to himself, resigned, already defeated, he would signal the projectionist to roll it. The lights would dim. The newsreel would begin. The old man would slump off the stage and trudge back up the aisle to his tiny, cluttered office behind the candy counter to count his quarters.

Out in the theater, the chaos would start slowly and eventually reign supreme—a chaos I'd known all my moviegoing life—a chaos incubated and sustained by row after row of my round-headed, buzz-cut, baby boom peers. Whoopee cushions blatted. Rubber band slingshots twanged. Jujubes flew. One especially raucous Saturday, in the middle of an old Roy Rogers movie, a chocolate-covered cherry splatted against the screen, hitting Trigger on his giant Technicolor ass and oozing down. The stain remained there for years. I remember Vivien Leigh flouncing through it when they rereleased *Gone with the Wind*. Spilled, syrupy, ten-cent-a-cup vending machine soft drinks ran in rivulets down the sloped floor under the seats, and we tracked the sticky residue up the once luxuriously carpeted aisles to the art deco men's room, where someone always clogged the urinal with heavy brown paper towels.

So there I was, sitting, behaving myself, awash in the noise and the churn, watching yet another cowboy movie. The good guys had the bad guys pinned down in the rocks up a box canyon, and everyone was shooting it out yet again. Somebody—one of the good guys—sighted his rifle and pulled the trigger, and a bad guy jumped up, grabbed his belly, and fell dead.

Between television and the Liberty Theater, I had witnessed this scene hundreds of times before, but for some reason, sitting there that day, I was suddenly aware that I would die some day. The news arrived with a jolt, and it was not easy to accept.

I had always thought of God and Jesus as good guys, as biblical versions of Roy Rogers or Hopalong Cassidy. They wore white robes if not white hats. And according to the nuns, God and Jesus stood up for the little guys. They suffered little children to come unto them. Sitting there in the dark, now aware I too would die, I thought either God and Jesus had double-crossed the nuns or the nuns were in on it and had double-crossed me.

Not that it made any difference. No matter how much I believed, no matter how hard I prayed, we were all going to die—every kid in the room. I remember turning away from the screen, looking up at the once classy, now dusty fleur-de-lis sconces on the theater walls and dreading absolutely everything.

There was always a point in those old cowboy movies when somebody out scouting gets down off his horse, crawls on his belly to the edge of a cliff, peeks over, and realizes the good guys are about to ride into an ambush. He comes back, riding hell-bent for leather, waving his hat, yelling, "Go back. It's a trick."

I wanted to ride back and warn the guys in the theater that it was all one big ambush. Everything—life, fun, matinees, Jujubes—was just a setup. Go back. It's a trick. But what good would warning them do? We were already in this world, and there was only one way out. So I kept my mouth shut. For that after-noon at least, death was my own little horror.

It was the darkest moment of my life so far. Eventually, the good guys roped the rustlers and Roy kissed Dale Evans. The two of them rode off into the sunset on a buckboard, the movie flick-ered to an end, and we all jostled out into the late afternoon light and went home. The initial jolt subsided. We grew up and went our separate ways.

For years there, I was too busy living to think much about my own mortality. If I remembered death at all, it came to me as a quick little reminder—a couple synapses while shaving or a blip on the verge of a night's sleep. It was one of those "oh, yeah, for-got about that" moments, a note to myself—like an appointment I made long ago and forgot to jot down on the calendar.

Lately, though, Death is starting to worm away at me again. It's getting a little more insistent, taking on the tone they use in overdue utility bills. Some days, reading the obits, I feel like the slowest wildebeest in the herd. Death is the hyena snapping at my heels. It's already brought down a few of the guys, and one of these days, well...

I hold death at bay with the memory of the old man from the Liberty Theater, long dead himself now, in church at nine o'clock mass on Sunday morning. He is wearing his nicer, less-rumpled blue Sunday suit. He is kneeling back on his hams, hands clasped, eyes screwed shut in prayer. God's light is falling around him. I can't tell if he's praying for salvation or better-behaved young matinee patrons.

Meanwhile, up on the altar, the deaf old parish priest, also dead these many years, is warning us all to behave or God will stop showing the kind of movies we like.

The Man on the Raft

We were sitting on the swimming raft at the lake—ten or twelve of us, a cross-section of the town's adolescent male population. Twelve-, thirteen-, and fourteen-year-olds too young for part-time summer work with a long afternoon to kill.

"I'm going to the lake, Ma. The guys'll be there."

Lake Coming of Age, where slightly older, more mysterious girls—girls who would be sophomores at high school that fall—spread their towels and lay in the sun, smelling of cocoa butter and baby oil, listening to Top 40 songs on a transistor radio.

Maybe boys their age had an easier time finding summer work (stocking store shelves or pumping gas). Maybe these girls came from slightly better-off families. Whatever it was, they were there every day. Their mothers' cars, windows rolled down, shimmered in the heat in the parking lot, beyond where we'd dropped our bikes when we'd come skidding up to the beach.

Farther down the beach, young matrons clustered blankets and set up base camps from which they supervised small children who dug, played, and swam near the swing set. The women sat, dispensing Kool-Aid from thermoses, arbitrating kid tiffs, endlessly counting heads, emitting an invisible but powerful wave that pushed us away from the shallow area inside the ropes where their children were playing. Adolescent boys. Yuk.

The sunbathing sirens added invisible repulsion waves of their own. They felt our ogling and leering even when lying there

35

on their towels on their stomachs, heads on arms with their eyes closed. Adolescent boys. Yuk.

The repulsion had forced us off the beach. We'd swum the sixty yards out to the raft and, after a bit of pushing and shoving—roughhousing quelled by the lifeguard via bullhorn—we'd settled down. Now we were sitting on the edge of the raft, ankles in the water, sharing information we'd gleaned about how the adult world worked and what was going on among our peers.

It was out there on the raft that summer that someone finally killed the rumor about the condom machine in the Phillips 66 station men's room. Since at least fifth grade, the word had been that if you put in your quarter and twisted the knob, a bell would ring and the attendant would come and make sure you were old enough to buy a condom—and that you were married.

But that summer, one of the guys screwed his courage to the sticking point, paid his money, and took his chances. No attendant had come, and the next day he'd swum the foil-wrapped Red Rooster brand condom out to the raft to prove it. We passed it around. We inspected it. The invisible repulsion wave from shore seemed to increase palpably.

When the temperature or the tedium rose on days like this, games of tag or hide-and-seek or tennis ball catch would break out. You could swim under the raft and, holding onto the anchor rope, hang there in the middle of a school of sunfish, the water cool, green, and clear all around.

Or you could take a deep breath and pull yourself twelve feet down the anchor rope to the bottom, where the water was even cooler, and holding yourself down with the anchor rope, you could sit there on a sunken fifty-five-gallon drum and contemplate life's mysteries for as long as your air lasted.

Why did the older girls lie there smelling of cocoa butter and baby oil if they didn't want to get ogled?

If the gas station attendant wasn't monitoring condom sales and local morality, who was?

You sat down there like Rodin's *The Thinker* in the cold, dark silence. You pondered.

One summer evening after supper, the year before, a six-year-old walked into the lake over the edge of a drop-off and disappeared. The mother was frantic. Other mothers held her and tried to comfort her.

"My baby," she yelled over and over again. "My baby. My baby."

The lifeguard had us line up, join hands, and walk out as far as we could, then turn around and walk back toward shore again, feeling for the child with our feet as we came. We couldn't find him. Someone made a phone call, and the volunteer fire whistle sounded. After a while, the volunteer fire department emergency team came. It took more than an hour to find the body. Sitting on the drum, pondering things, you could feel the dead child floating in the now amniotic lake, hanging there, watching you.

Eventually, you shot back up to the sunlight and the heat and the raft noise. You climbed up onto the raft and found a place among the guys where you could sit with your ankles in the water and watch the girls and their cocoa butter and baby oil shine and shimmer in the heat on the beach.

So there we were that afternoon, sitting on the edge of the raft, when an unfamiliar car pulled into the lot—a young guy's car, a two-door Chevy with fender skirts and burbling glass-packed mufflers, a car too expensive for one of the older high school kids who bullied us on sight. And besides, this time of day older high school kids were working.

The driver slid the car into a parking spot in the shade of a huge old willow, killed the engine, and got out. He carried his beach stuff rolled up in a towel, and he walked through the maze of cast-aside bicycles. He stood for a moment surveying the beach while everyone on the beach surveyed him.

There was something of a "that's right, look me over" swagger to him. He was a handsome guy with an almost-too-perfect haircut, maybe twenty, still teen-age trim but growing into his frame.

He was wearing a white, tight-legged swimsuit that showed him off. Looking back now, I can see he'd put some thought into his appearance—something not many young men did in those days. He was a carefully arranged young Adonis, a latter-day James Dean, a Sal Mineo, or maybe a Montgomery Clift.

He was a slightly affected blue-collar fashion statement. He looked like he should have been working on a factory floor, as if maybe he'd talked some good-hearted girl coworker into clocking off for him, then slipped out a side door and snuck away for the afternoon.

Back then, in the small ads at the back of car magazines, they used to sell license plate–shaped signs to hang below the bumper of chopped and channeled street rods. "No club," one plate read. "Lone Wolf." I had seen the ads in the magazines in the library at school and wondered what kind of guy might be out there, cruising the highways alone, a wanderer, a rebel without a cause, a tattoo on his chest and that plate on his back bumper.

Maybe this guy. Then again, maybe not. Even at this distance, there was something a bit too precious, affected, and strange about him.

When you looked at him you didn't hear the call of the open road. You imagined the duplex he rented halfway up a dead-end street behind a factory somewhere like North Chicago. Here, you sensed, was a slightly too old, restless youth struggling with decades of dull, drab existence yet to come—youth not so much smoldering as moldering under the weight of the mundane. You looked at him and you imagined the half-eaten pack of bologna, the four-day-old loaf of Wonder bread, and the nearly empty jar of Miracle Whip on the shelf of the small Frigidaire in the duplex kitchen.

Anyhow, he let all of us—young matrons, sunbathing high school girls, and the guys out on the raft, everyone—take a good look. The only people who didn't check him out were the young kids on the swings and splashing in the shallow water. Then he walked past the sunbathing girls, through our towels and high-topped basketball shoes, to a vacant patch of sand on a slight incline where he flapped his towel open, arranged his beach stuff, and sat down. He stripped off his shirt, found a bottle of baby oil, greased himself up, ran his hands through his hair, and lay back to soak up the sun.

A sleepy, small-town, middle-of-the-summer, middle-of-the-afternoon normalcy seemed to return. The young matrons began talking among themselves again, counting heads, sending new waves of repulsion in our direction. The sunbathing girls who had looked up to watch the Lone Wolf pass dropped their heads back down onto their folded arms. Out on the raft, we went back to talking, ogling at a distance, and taking dips to cool off.

Everything was going along the way it always did until the Lone Wolf sat up, stretched, stood up, and walked down to the water. He waded out until he was hip deep, and he stood there, twenty feet from where the kid had walked over the edge of the drop-off, plashing handfuls of water onto his chest, getting used to it. Then he dove and started to swim for the raft.

He swam with that efficient, slow, rhythmic stroke good swimmers have. The one that gets them where they're going faster than it looks like it should. On the beach, with that perfect haircut, he had looked like a post–high school biker hood. But hoods couldn't swim like this guy could. Hoods wouldn't go to the beach at all if they could help it.

If he wasn't a hood, what was he? We watched him coming toward us with apprehension. The raft was kid turf, one of those places adults just didn't go—like the underside of the railroad viaduct over the river where we dropped down between the tracks and the timbers to smoke cigarettes we'd stolen from our fathers, or beneath the highway bridge over the river where we cached the old dirty magazines we sometimes found along the road. There was an unspoken agreement. No one over fourteen or female generally allowed. Not under the viaduct, not under the highway bridge, and not out on the raft. No one over fourteen or female would want to have been out there with us anyhow.

But here came the Lone Wolf, oddly cool and confident. Suddenly he was there, first pulling himself up the ladder onto the raft, then standing there, flipping his head to one side, his hair falling into place, a too-easy Pepsodent smile on his face. And then he sat down, reclining on one elbow like Adam on the ceiling of the Sistine Chapel, half-sitting, half-leaning against the upshafts of the ladder.

It was a singularly peculiar pose. It looked studied and awkward and straining to be casual. We weren't the most perceptive people in town, but we could sense he was trying to show us something. And eventually, each of us saw what it was protruding from the left leg of his swimsuit.

I don't remember him saying a word or even acknowledging us. He just posed, knee cocked, elbow on knee, hand elegantly poised. He posed and pretended to be unaware of the intruding protrusion.

"I don't think he was an old guy. He was older than we were, probably about twenty," my brother e-mailed me when I asked him about the incident recently. "A bit of a dude judging by his hairstyling. He wore a tight-fitting suit, swam out to and sat on the raft, leaning against the ladder rail while we huddled at the other end. There was no eye contact.

"His member poked out along his leg. We had to jump into the lake and swim away to get out of his hearing to talk about him—and it. We probably went back to the raft just to confirm it.

"He was unknown to us, which is remarkable because the town was so small that everyone knew everyone."

There was a sandbar maybe fifteen yards from the raft—a place where you could stand in three and a half feet of water. I remember some of the guys swimming over there to consult. I remember treading deeper water, too, talking with the kid who lived three doors down the block. We were two round heads and two sets of kid shoulders bobbing in the lake, and we were both amused and confused. Here was something a kid didn't see every day. A guy—an adult for all practical purposes—with his unit poking out of the leg of his swimming suit, a guy just lying there among us, relaxed, cool as a cucumber.

I don't remember anyone being shocked. There was no talk of swimming in and telling the lifeguard. But once you'd left the raft, once you'd adjourned to the sandbar to discuss the situation, you couldn't climb back on. Poised and posed as he was, the Lone Wolf was gate-keeping the ladder.

A nervous game of tag broke out around and under the raft. Our hearts weren't in it. We were just killing time, waiting for the Lone Wolf to leave. At one point, I took a deep breath and dove down the anchor rope to mull things over.

For a moment, the length of that breath, we were a triangle—the dead kid, the Lone Wolf, and me. I was connected to a world where children drowned after supper on beautiful summer evenings and a world where perverse little men performed perverse little acts. In the middle of infinity, on the bottom of a lake, on the verge of adulthood—or at least a more sophisticated adolescence—it was a moment of semienlightenment. Then it was time to go up for air.

"He eventually left and never was seen again," my brother's e-mail concludes. Decades came and went. So did people. Life happened. The whole incident disappeared. Then, one night, on the verge of sleep, somewhere in middle age, there was the Lone Wolf again, recumbent on the raft, exposed, a blast from the past, pleased as hell with himself.

"I shall be telling this with a sigh / Somewhere ages and ages hence," writes Robert Frost. Well, there. It's told. And somewhere an old woman is still mourning that child. And somewhere the Lone Wolf is eating a bologna sandwich and thinking about going for a swim.

Lawnmower Repair

The neighbor was trying to start his lawnmower. No soap. The thing was dead.

"Why don't you start it the way my dad starts ours?" my son suggested.

"How's that?" the neighbor asked.

"He kicks it and says, '#$%**&*.'"

I hail from a long line of mechanical Neanderthals, from people fundamentally cross-threaded for mechanics. Other men reach for just the right box wrench and loosen bolts deftly. I can never find the right wrench, so I crimp on an oversized pair of vice grips and inevitably round the top of the bolt to the point where it will be stuck there for eternity. Either that or I apply enough pressure to make the obstinate bolt give way all at once, slamming my knuckles into some nearby flange, drawing blood and a few minutes of "#$%**&*."

Not for me the satisfaction that comes with knowledge, aptitude, competence, tenacious patience, and maturity. No. I learned everything I know about home mechanics from my father—including "#$%**&*."

At our house, the tools were kept in an old metal box—a tin thing maybe twenty inches long, a foot wide, and ten inches deep. It was designed to look like a wicker picnic hamper, with little paintings in a faux early automobile motif. But there was no holiday in the offing when that thing came out.

There was a sixteenth of an inch of oily grit on the bottom— iron filings and rust and gunk from projects past. The tools themselves were remarkably bad. A mixture of woodworking and mechanic's devices, they were cheap, chipped, and rusting. Loose-jointed, mismatched, and diabolically malevolent. There were razor blades in there and spools of rusty wire and errant nails and tacks and stiff wire brushes to poke holes in your fingertips as you rummaged around. Surely tetanus lurked only an errant eighth of an inch away as you poked your pudgy little fingers in, stirring the muck, hoping the right bolt, nut, or screw would churn up.

Then there was what was not in there—the right-sized socket, ratchet, screwdriver, or wrench. Whatever you needed was almost sure to be missing, no doubt hiding somewhere out in the lawn, where someone dropped it after making a quick bike repair and pedaling off. Not to worry. More often than not you would find it later, usually by running over it with the lawnmower.

We Smiths started any project at a disadvantage, three steps behind any other kid on the block, with the wrong tool or a broken tool and a bad attitude. Looking back now, I can see I approached those jobs the way I played high school nose tackle. Every project was an opponent, something to be subdued as quickly and aggressively as possible.

"Take that, you #$%**&*."

Nor are Smiths graced with great manual dexterity. We lack fine motor skills. To watch us work is to want to reach in and take over, to take the project out of our bumbling hands. We spent our formative years trying to reach in and take over from one another. It was not a good thing to do if whoever was holding the tool had had time to work himself into a frenzy of frustration.

And so it went for years. Engine adjustments and carburetor tweaks befuddled us—especially those involving needle valves. If the manual recommended seating the valve completely, then opening it a quarter turn to the left, we would somehow find ourselves going two and a quarter turns. Two and a quarter led to five. Eventually the entire #$%**&! mechanism would fly out of its seat, disassemble in midair, and come to rest under the workbench, way back under the workbench where you couldn't reach it on your hands and knees. You had to lie on your stomach and poke at it with the handle end of the push broom.

All these skills we learned from my father, a smallish, intelligent, introspective man who applied his own logic to home repair projects. Not for him the simple, straightforward thinking that allowed the human race to come down out of the trees and invent civilizations. My father was a thinking man, and thinking required a certain left-handed, outside the box, Rube Goldberg approach to home repair and maintenance. If he couldn't get the result he wanted with whatever tool fell under his hand, he resorted to some tenuous repair or patch, to miles of electrician's tape or buckets of Bondo and La Brea–sized pits of epoxy glue. When he made a home repair, the repair might not be pretty, but it would be permanent.

He would stand there and admire his handiwork: the glue- or tape-swollen handle of some household object, the flickering picture on the television with a new tube from the drugstore, or the electrical cord on a table lamp with its new knot of electrician's tape making it look like a python that had just swallowed a pig. "When Smith fixes them," he would say with no small amount of satisfaction, "they stay fixed."

When all else failed on an internal combustion project—and it usually did—my father would take his victim apart and, a piece at a time, wash all its components in a coffee can of gasoline. The reluctant-to-start three-and-a-half horse Tecumseh engine on the family lawnmower underwent this procedure at least once a summer for quite a while.

He never mowed the lawn, so he never started the mower. He did not know there was a trick—indeed, several tricks—to it. You took three pulls with the throttle in the choke position and three pulls with the throttle wide open. You gave it a couple of #$%**&*s and a properly placed kick, and it lurched reluctantly to life. Not knowing the trick, coming across one of us in the middle of the process, oblivious to any effort to explain the process to him, my father would misdiagnose the problem and start tearing the engine down and cleaning its parts.

The sight of the man and the toolbox and the lawnmower and a coffee can of gasoline in the driveway on Saturday morning was enough to make us all try to slink away unnoticed. Being his largest and slowest child, I was the one most often spotted as I tried to disappear behind the fence. I was the one most often pressed into service on his repair jobs.

To this day, I cringe when I hear the words, "C'mere. Gimme a hand." I have nightmares about helping him bitch up the already tentative mechanics of that lawnmower.

"Hand me the #$%**&* pincher pliers," he would say, "pincher pliers" being the family term for vice grips. I would hand him the #$%**&* pincher pliers, and in no time at all, bolts would start plinking into the coffee can with its gasoline. There did not appear to be any particular reason why he chose those particular bolts. Nor did they seem to need to be cleaned. Later in life, I would spend two years running motor pools for the U.S. Army. I worked with seasoned professional mechanics every day. These were master sergeants approaching retirement who'd spent decades in automotive repair working on jeeps, trucks, and tanks. At no point in those two years did I hear one of those men say, "Well, there's your problem right there, sir. Dirty #$%**&* bolts."

In the driveway on those Saturday mornings, mine was not to reason why. Mine was to stand there, waiting, stubbing a toe in the dirt, handing him the #$%**&* this, digging the #$%**&* that out of that viscous tool box, taking the heat for the missing seven-sixteenths-inch socket, silently questioning the wisdom of disconnecting the carburetor linkage, rusty cable still attached and under some springlike tension, from the carburetor itself.

It was as stressful as it would have been to watch him perform surgery on the family dog. For all its eccentricities, the lawnmower was a loyal machine. I was on good terms with it. If I observed protocol, administered the prescribed number of starter pulls in the right order with the throttle in the right sequence of positions, followed by just the right kick and a properly intoned #$%**&*, the machine started (albeit reluctantly) and worked just fine for me. Now here was the old man unbolting bolts, backing off set screws, taking a wire brush to the spark plug, taking the lawnmower's very life in his hands. Disaster lurked everywhere. I spotted parts, couplings, and bolts he had not yet noticed and prayed his gaze would not fall on them.

"Hide, little gas line hose," I would urge behind his back. Or, "Lay low, starter rope retriever mechanism." I have colluded with inanimate lawnmower parts behind my father's back.

At some point, an hour or two into the procedure, Saturday lunch hoving into sight, having found nothing seriously wrong with the patient, and equipped with a coffee can full of gasoline and an assortment of impeccably clean bolts, washers, and other parts, he would reverse the process and start closing the patient. Things would get reattached. Sometimes smoothly, sometimes with a bit of cross-threading, bolts would get reseated and torqued too tightly. The spark plug would undergo one last inspection and one more wipe with his handkerchief. Then it, too, would get cross-threaded, backed off, and ultimately reseated. The foam rubber air filter got rinsed in gasoline, wrung, and put back into place.

The job finally done, he would try to start it. Pull after pull, nothing would happen. When he and his patience tired, he would turn to me.

"#$%**&*," he would say. "You try it."

And I would go through the timeless ritual. Three pulls with the throttle in the choke position. Three pulls with the throttle wide open. A kick. A "#$%**&*!"

And the lawnmower would reluctantly return from its near-death experience. "Sput," it would go. "Sput…sput…sput…" And I would lunge for the throttle and find a setting where it wasn't gargling gasoline. "Sputtety-sputtety-sput," it would mutter somewhat irascibly. Another small throttle adjustment and a couple of turns to the right on a set screw on the carburetor, and it would find its pace and timing and overcome whatever my father and I had done to it.

"There," my father would say. "Sounds better, doesn't it? Put the tools away. Let's have some lunch."

Lunch would be Oscar Mayer summer sausage on Wonder bread with yellow mustard and often a decorative whorl of lawnmower gunk where we'd peeled back the bread to daub on the mustard without first washing our hands.

To him it was quality time. To me it was hell. Now I have visited the other side of the equation. A father myself, I have pressed my own children into service on projects like this. I have sensed them standing there, attuned too precisely to my moods in that unspoken judgmental way I had with my father in his driveway. I have piled fumbling mistake on top of mistake and single-handedly made matters worse not just for the lawnmower but for the kid. And as I did, I have heard my father's voice coming from somewhere.

"Wash the bolts," it says. "Wash the #$%**&* bolts."

The Biscayne

Somewhere in a junkyard in Lake County, Illinois, my father's once-tan, nine-passenger, 1962 Chevrolet Biscayne station wagon sits rusting and moldering. Any usable parts are long gone, including the wheels, carburetor, generator, pumps, radiator, headlights, radio, and anything else forty years of backyard mechanics might have needed to fix their own Chevrolets. The demand for 1962 Chevrolet parts has abated. Grass—and maybe even a small northern Illinois hawthorn tree—is probably growing up through the engine compartment and floorboards.

The front bumper is no doubt gone, but I'm fairly sure the back one is still there. There was that tear in it where the hook on the end of Wayne Kick's tow truck cable tore through the chrome when, in our youth and innocence, working twelve feet below the surface of Lake Minear, brother number three and I hooked onto the bumper instead of the frame of the car, then shot to the surface and told Wayne to hit it. But I'm getting ahead of myself.

My father bought the station wagon virtually new from a mechanic who worked for Wayne's father, Sid. Sid Kick owned the gas station, and he'd had my father's business for years. There must have been something turbulent going on behind the scenes, because Sid changed brands several times over the years. He was Texaco when I learned to read. He was Conoco for a while, then Citgo, if I remember correctly, and I think he may have given up

48

on the majors altogether by the time I left for college and lost track of his operation.

He wore blue or green twill Sears, Roebuck work clothes and completed the look with a grease-stained hat, the kind worn by the singing Men of Texaco on Milton Berle's television show. He wore the hat and the vaguely preoccupied look of a man juggling details. In those days, before credit cards, regular customers could charge gas at Sid's—"Put it on the cuff." Often, Sid and his staff might fuel five or six customers' cars between trips to the office to jot transactions down. I would guess that between filling tanks, washing windshields, running the tabs, keeping whatever oil company whose sign he'd hung over his station that year at bay, supervising whatever mechanics were on the payroll that month, and keeping an eye on his inventory of minor parts (wiper blades, spark plugs), Sid had plenty to distract himself with. To talk to Sid was to try to insinuate yourself into the ongoing conversation he was already having with himself.

You could learn quite a bit about auto mechanics and manhood hanging around the repair bays at Kick's. How to read a greasy lubrication chart, locate all the fittings, and take a grease gun to a car. How to change oil. How to hot-patch an inner tube, plug a flat tire, set ignition points, and clean and gap spark plugs. How to use a timing light. Perhaps most important of all, how to swear like a mechanic who'd just had an unfortunate encounter with a hot exhaust manifold.

There were other things to learn, too. Sid's brother Harry, a simpler, more childlike, and less preoccupied version of Sid himself, worked at the station. Every so often, he would roll up his green twill sleeve and show us the fading, wrinkling, pre–World War II hula girl tattoo on his right forearm and make her dance by clenching his fist and rolling his knuckles.

Back then, before lawyers, a kid could walk around the service bays. You could stand under the hoist and look up at a drive train and the rest of the undercarriage of whatever car they had overhead. You could lean over a fender, peer down through the wheel well, and ask a mechanic on a creeper below, "Whatcha doin'?" More often than not the mechanic would take the time to tell you. They appeared to be gruff, conflicted, and unrefined men in blue jeans and black engineer boots—men like Marlon Brando in *The Wild Ones*. But they were generous with their time and patient. Even as they worked, they would explain things to you and answer your questions more than thoroughly—to the point where you became bored and walked away.

We were at Sid Kick's a lot because the family cars were at Sid Kick's a lot. My father's tastes in automobiles ran the gauntlet from eclectic to downright eccentric, and decades before computerized ignitions and fuel-injected engines, one of his cars always needed work.

It was there, at Sid Kick's, no doubt waiting for a repair, that my father first laid eyes on the station wagon. One of the mechanics had custom ordered it and had taken delivery only a few weeks earlier. Then he had had second thoughts. He only had two children. What did he need all that room for? My father, on the other hand, had nine children and a wife. Even if it was two passenger seats short of being big enough for his family, it would be eminently more practical than anything he owned. And the mechanic didn't want to keep making the car payments. A motivated seller met a motivated buyer. I'm sure my father bailed the mechanic out, taking out a car loan to pay off the mechanic's car loan plus whatever the down payment had been. I'm sure the deal was fair and square for the other guy. My father was the worst car buyer in Lake County.

Strange, because he was a great card player. He played bridge on the train on the way to work every morning and penny ante poker on the way home at night. He used to take enough money out of the poker games to pay for his monthly train ticket, and on occasions when the Chicago press went on the road to cover a story, he was heavily favored to win the nightly gin rummy game in the hotel bar. But he was no good at buying or selling cars. He seems to have been born with an unfortunate birthmark only car salesmen could read—a birthmark that evidently said, "Please fleece me." They could see that "gotta have it today" look in his eye and played him like a dime-store kazoo. By the time the Biscayne arrived in our lives, even my brothers and I could read him. We could sense that new car urge building in him for weeks. He'd begin to slow down as he drove past car dealerships and stole obvious looks at certain cars on the lot. Slumped in adolescent embarrassment beside him, we could see the salesmen standing behind the big plate glass windows, rocking back and forth on their heels, hands in their pockets, jingling their change, watching him, muttering to one another, biding their time but chalking up the sale against this month's sales contest.

When the day finally came, he walked in having to have it, unable to walk away, eager to get fleeced on some absolute embarrassment—new or used. There was a hulking old 1952 Chrysler New Yorker with both an automatic transmission and a clutch that we nicknamed the "Whale." It was huge and green and born of that era after the war but before tail fins. It had been elegant at some point, with room for five or six of us in the backseat. The once-plush upholstery was full of human dander, and it had those granny straps hanging from the doorposts. The Whale threw a rod on the way into town one evening—a form of internal combustion suicide, I guess. The car was depressed—once so elegant, but fallen so far.

There was a rusted out Willys-Overland jeep. The rocker panels were gone, the paint riddled with rust blisters. We still refer to this era as Pop's Bondo period. The jeep had a standard transmission on the steering column, and if you threw it from first to second or second to third in just the right rhythm, you didn't have to use the clutch. Then there were a couple of Model A Fords—more hobbies than transportation—which he used to impart his left-handed brand of automotive mechanics to us. For a while there, he became a Mercury man. The local Mercury dealer had gone to high school with my mother, and I guess my father thought that meant the man would give him some sort of a deal. I doubt the man ever did. You don't get to own a car dealership by giving deals to the husbands of your high school classmates. Especially to men who seemed more than willing to pay full retail and who felt they'd driven a hard bargain in the process.

Not that it mattered to us. Bargains or not, the cars he bought from the man were still Mercurys. What were Mercurys anyhow? Nothing but Fords for Republicans, poor men's Buicks. Mercury hadn't made a decent car since the early fifties. Even with those Mercs, you had to chop and channel them and add fender skirts, Continental kits, and lurid blue-pink brake lights—a style far too young and cool for a man like Pop.

One night, he came home with a white, four-door, six-cylinder Mercury Comet—one of Detroit's first stabs at a compact economy car. It was an underpowered, basic, no self-esteem little machine with neither pickup nor panache, a glamourless object with the soul of a Nash Rambler.

The only fond memory I can dredge up about the Comet was the night I rode along as my father taught my brother how to drive on the Tri-State Tollway. My brother pulled up to an automated tollbooth, tossed some coins toward the hopper, started to pull ahead, then realized he was a nickel light on the toll. He backed up, tossed in the nickel, and as the gate went up, he stepped on the gas, forgetting the car was still in reverse. It was one of the happiest moments of my childhood.

The Comet was a four-door embarrassment, and when my mother stopped dead on an Edens Expressway on-ramp and someone hit her, totaling the Comet, we secretly celebrated. We hoped my father would replace it with something sportier. When he came home with the station wagon from Kick's, we were as crestfallen as he was proud—and he was beaming. He'd gotten a good deal on a car for once, a car big enough to fit the family. Just think—all eleven of us could go somewhere *together* in one car, eight facing forward, three in the rear-facing third seat. Think of it. We could go together to visit relatives or on a family vacation to northern Wisconsin.

My father raised the hood and showed us the engine. The mechanic had specified General Motors' reliable 283 V-8—a middle-of-the-line piece of equipment for most car owners but a definite step up for us. Two hundred and eighty-three cubic inches. Hot damn. Real power. In a straight stoplight drag race, the station wagon would have walked the Comet, even with all eleven of us aboard.

The car had a transistor radio, too. We didn't have to wait for it to warm up any more. Just turn it on, and there would be WLS or WJJD—Chicago's Top 40 rock-and-roll stations—pumping out adolescence's soundtrack. We'd turn it on, and the music would blare for as long as it took my father to reach over and turn the radio off. Click—blare. Click—silence. When my father was behind the wheel, the radio delivered news on the hour from WGN or White Sox baseball. Nothing else. We were left to amuse ourselves in silence, to stare moodily out the window at the world passing by, to contemplate the sins of our past lives.

There could be no doubt about it, though. That first night, standing there in his crushed limestone driveway in front of his home, surrounded by his wife and children, my father was mightily pleased with his new station wagon and with himself. So much so, that only a few weeks later, with the odometer still well under three thousand miles, he piled us all in and took us up to northern Wisconsin for that vacation.

We washed and vacuumed the car the night before, right down to scouring the white sidewalls on the tires. We clamped on a cartop carrier, and we loaded it and covered it with a tarp. All we would have to do in the morning would be to get up and go, which we did. We were on our way before dawn, the station wagon riding low on its springs. We must have looked like latter-day Joads.

My mother and father were up front, with one kid between them and the baby of the family in cloth diapers on my mother's lap. We three oldest boys took the middle seat and passed the second-youngest child back and forth from knee to knee and lap to lap. The middle three kids took the rear-facing backseat and amused themselves by waving to people in other cars and pumping their fists up and down to get truck drivers to honk their air horns. There were no seat belts.

Things were going beautifully. It was all new-car smell and eager anticipation of a week in the pine-scented north woods. The engine purred. The hundred or so miles from our house to Madison may well have been the high-water mark for my father as a car-owning family man. He was seeing the USA in his Chevrolet. Yes, sir, life didn't get any better than that.

Then, as we made our way through Madison, someone side-swiped us. Who knows? Maybe the kids in the backseat distracted him. My father pulled over, got out, went back, talked to the guy. It was silent inside the car. Those of us facing forward turned and craned our necks to observe the confrontation. After a certain amount of give-and-take, my father returned to the car, and we resumed the drive north, all of us the slightest bit more glum. We had long since learned to gauge his anger by his body language. He was at the stage where he breathed heavily through his nose, making the hairs there whistle.

The long, deep scratch in the paint on the left-rear quarter panel would be there forever, but we were on vacation. Our mood brightened slightly as we headed north on Highway 51, en route to a cabin on a beautiful north woods lake in a car that, in spite of the baby in cloth diapers up front, still smelled like a new car. Someone in the rear-facing backseat began to sing "Ninety-Nine Bottles of Beer on the Wall." Someone in the middle told them to shut up or they'd get pounded. By Stevens Point, we were back to normal, the accident more or less forgotten.

Then somewhere south of Wausau, someone in the far backseat threw up. It was the Asian flu, and just like that it was so long, new-car smell. We pulled over, ministered to whoever it was who had hurled, and resumed the trek. Twenty miles later, one or two of the weaker-stomached among us succumbed to the flu or the powers of negative thinking and threw up, too. The trip became a death march—stop and clean up, start, stop and clean up, change clothes, start again. It was midafternoon by the time we limped into the resort. The theme for the week had been established.

The cabin felt like a World War I Spanish flu army hospital ward as the virus made its way through the family. No one fished. No one camped. Everyone lolled around reading the Zane Grey paperbacks and old *Reader's Digests* that came with the cabin. Those who were on the mend nursed those who were getting sick. There was one underplumbed bathroom, and as soon as someone raced in and latched the door, someone else would need to race in, too. When the week mercifully ended, we strapped our luggage to the station wagon roof, helped our sick into the car, and swooned back down through Wisconsin only to get rear-ended yet again in Madison.

It was the end of the station wagon as a new car but the beginning of its long and exceptional tour of family duty. Five of us learned to drive in that car. There were years of daily trips to and from the commuter train station. Lord only knows the gross tonnage of groceries my mother hauled home from the Jewel Food Store in it. My older brother and I double-dated in it. It was all Bobby Vinton and "Blue Velvet" and getting home three minutes past curfew.

On big nights (proms, homecoming, what have you), if you played your cards right and arranged everyone's schedule just so, you could sometimes even have it for a solo date. It was a passion pit Saturday night and a church taxi Sunday morning. The miles and the years rolled by, and that middle-of-the-line station wagon did what Detroit designed and built it to do for our big, middle-class family in the middle of the country.

It was utilitarian. You could put the backseats down and haul stuff. My father even had a small rowboat that fit back there.

After supper on summer evenings, we would help him put the boat in the car, and he would go down to Lake Minear, a flooded gravel pit lined with volunteer box elders and lachrymal willows, to fish for an hour or two before dark. Sometimes he would invite one of us to go with him. Sometimes he would take my mother along.

This was, in many ways, the high point of his life. His career was going well. He had everything under control. There were college tuition bills on the horizon, but life was good. On warm summer evenings, if he played his cards right, he could escape the crowded house for an hour or two anyhow.

He had his whole boat-launching technique down to a science. He'd back the station wagon down the boat ramp, throw it in park, get out, and go around to the tailgate. He would slide the boat out—oars, fishing tackle, rods, and all—then go park the car and go fishing. With more than ninety thousand miles on it by then, the station wagon was old, reliable, tried-and-true.

One night though, one fateful night, my father backed down the ramp, threw the wagon into park, and stepped out and around to the tailgate only to find the car rolling into the lake. My mother was along on the trip. She'd gotten out of the car earlier and was watching from a dock near the ramp.

He raced back to the wheel and stepped on the brakes, hoping to arrest the momentum. But the rear end of the car was already floating, and the front brakes alone couldn't stop it from sliding into the water. He closed the door, threw the car into gear, and gunned the engine, hoping somehow to propel the car back toward dry land. No use. The front wheels were still on shore, but the rest of the car was picking up momentum, and like a just-launched ocean liner, it was drifting ever so tentatively out to sea. Sensing futility, he tried to open the door and get out, but the water pressure outside the car made that impossible. So he dove through the open driver's side window, climbed up on the hood, sat there, took off his shoes and socks, and threw them to shore. He and his station wagon were perhaps forty feet out by then.

"Can you swim in from there?" my mother, a nonswimmer, called anxiously.

He could and he did, and together on the dock, my parents watched as their station wagon continued out to sea another fifty feet or so, then slipped nose first, rear end high in the air like the *Titanic,* under the placid evening surface of Lake Minear. The ripples resolved themselves. Tranquility returned. The willows seemed a bit sadder somehow. Then the rowboat popped to the surface like Queequeg's coffin. A moment later, both oars appeared.

Two of us were in college by then, home for the summer, indolent youth lolling around, smoking cigarettes, when a neighbor came careening up the street in his car, honking his horn, squealing into our driveway. My father jumped out of the passenger's side, yelled for us, and gave us the news. My mother stepped out of the car with somewhat less urgency and went inside to call Kick's. Then all three older boys plus my father returned to the lake in the other family car.

He stood on the dock and directed us. We swam out, retrieved the boat and oars, and began diving to locate the sunken car. We found it, on its tires, in maybe fourteen feet of water, tailgate still down, rear end facing the shore. When Wayne Kick showed up, he backed his tow truck up to an oak tree and ran the boom cable through the fork of the tree down to the water's edge. We hooked it to the boat, ferried it out, swam it down to the car, hooked it onto the bumper, then shot to the surface and gave Wayne the thumbs-up sign and urged him to hit it.

As he coaxed the winch lever forward, the slack came out of the cable and the truck's big engine lugged down against the weight of the submerged car. Almost as quickly as it started, though, the engine revved up again, and Wayne let go of the lever. The hook had torn through the bumper.

So we went back to work, relaying the cable out to the car via the boat, taking it down. Hooking it through the frame of the car and back onto the cable itself was a bit more of a problem. It took several trips down and several trips back up for air, but eventually we got it done, and in the deepening twilight, Wayne hit the lever again. Like a huge snapping turtle, a few feet at a time, the Biscayne made its ponderous, submerged way to shore, then up the bank, where Wayne hooked it up and towed it off to the station to be dried out.

That car ran two more years and twenty thousand more miles. But it always smelled faintly like a sinus cavity full of weedy lake water. I was in the army halfway around the world when he traded it for something else. Something eccentric. I'm not sure what.

I own a little German car now—a high-mileage used car. But it's tight and precise and a guilty pleasure to drive. Sometimes, on the highway, I point a few of its features out to my long-dead father. Stuff I think he would have liked. He didn't like Germans so much after the war, but I think he would have liked this car.

When I open the hood and look down into the engine compartment to show his spirit around, I get the strangest feeling we're not at Sid Kick's any more. The engine is a cowled, fuel-injected monolith. There's a dipstick for the oil, a battery, and a radiator cap. There is little else I or the mechanics I knew back then might identify. It looks like it belongs in a modern art museum.

My older brother is gone now, too, but if I knew where that station wagon was, I'd grab my younger brother and go visit it. I'd kick around in the weeds, run a hand along the scratch in the left-rear quarter panel, stick my head in the window, and sniff for that weedy lake-water smell.

"You know, Pop," I'd say under my breath, "you got this one right."

A Visit to the Doctor

There was an ashtray on the desk in Dr. Day's examining room, a shallow brass dish with birds' heads, ibises or storks or something, their necks arched, the birds facing in opposite directions with beaks open so Dr. Day could wedge his Lucky Strike cigarette laterally across the bird's beak and let the bird hold it while he held a five-by-seven note card from your file with both hands and thought about you and whatever it was that had you perched up there on the examining table in the cloud of smoke behind him.

He was a bullet-headed, barrel-bodied little man in a Ben Casey smock that day in the autumn of 1962, almost fifty, a physician and surgeon out of one of the big land-grant schools down in Kansas. His crew cut undulated over and through rolls of fat on the back of his neck. Fat sagged, too, from the sides of his rib cage, down and out across the saddle of his lower back. The Eisenhower years had been good. Beef and potatoes every evening, and no doubt a toddy or two, had given the man the shape of a pear.

The Luckies were beginning to exact their toll. He had to pull a bit harder when he picked one out of a bird's beak and puffed. Every breath whistled on the way in, rolled around down there without much traction, and came out with a short, heavy, rheumy plop, as if someone had dropped a sack of wet sand on the floor from hip height.

His smock was light green and rayon—a color and texture that made you think of radium. What a coincidence. The X-rays (two of them) of my right knee clamped onto the light box on the wall to his left had me thinking of radium, too. The entire trip to Dr. Day's office set off some sort of internal Geiger counter that measured anxiety, and it was reaching dangerous levels in the cramped little room.

My pants were figure-eighted around my ankles. A towel sagged across my lap. My father, smoking too, was in the room, sitting on a straight chair beside Dr. Day's desk. My father never took us to the doctor unless it was something serious, and here he was, trying to keep the mood light. Dr. Day didn't seem to have a light mood. Not in the office. You had the idea he might enjoy a few cocktails and lead the Saturday night country club conga line now and then, but Monday through Friday, in and around medical matters, the man functioned at a low, steady, scientific drone. The Geiger counter ratcheted up a bit more.

Dr. Day hung his cigarette in the corner of his mouth, turned from his notes, and squinted through the smoke at the X-rays again. He tapped a blurry white-and-dark space behind the kneecap.

"Water on the knee," he said, the tone of his voice curt, full of that authority people afforded doctors and clergymen in those days. "Torn meniscus. Going to drain it, immobilize it, and see what happens."

He pressed a button to call the nurse.

"Football hero," my father said for Dr. Day's benefit.

"Season's over, Sport," Dr. Day said to me over his shoulder. He lit a new Lucky from the butt of the old one, spun around, and patted me on the knee. "This might hurt a little."

The nurse knocked on the door and stuck her head in. She looked frumpy and competent, like Hazel the maid in the *Saturday Evening Post* cartoon series.

"Yes, doctor?"

"Gonna drain this knee," Dr. Day said to her. "Set me up."

"Yes, doctor."

She went to a radium-green cabinet on the wall beside my father and took out a stainless steel tray and a small stainless steel bowl. She set the tray on the small counter beneath the cabinet, laid a white cotton towel on it, put the bowl on the towel, then opened the drawer and pulled out a big syringe. A very big syringe. She closed the drawer and opened the one immediately below it. There was a row of needles on a white towel arranged by length and gauge. She paused for a moment, then chose the last one on the right. The bastard must have been three and a half inches long.

She screwed the big syringe into the big needle and put it on the tray. This was before disposable syringes, and the setup was all glass and stainless steel. It looked like something from a mad scientist movie. It looked lethal. She added a bottle of alcohol and a bowl of cotton balls.

"Ready, Doctor."

"Hold him," Dr. Day told her.

The nurse put an arm around my shoulder. She was a small, wide woman. I was six feet tall and well past two hundred pounds by then. A Baby Huey. Had I keeled over, she would have been trapped. She looked worried, but she tried to look reassuring.

Dr. Day turned to my father. "I had Tommy Tower in here for the same thing last week. Fainted dead away."

The old man stubbed out his cigarette, picked a fleck of tobacco off his tongue, and accepted the information nonchalantly. He didn't go to football games. He didn't know Tommy Tower, varsity captain, college prospect, and the toughest kid in town. I did.

Still, something had to be done. I'd banged the knee during practice, and while getting ready to shower, I'd looked down and—damn. The knee had been huge, the size of a cantaloupe. I showed it to Coach, and he had me stand on the training table, and, my knee at his eye level, he tentatively poked at it. His finger disappeared into the meat up to the first knuckle. Damn. Coach had wrapped it in a used ACE bandage. I walked home on it, and by the time I got there it was the size of a small watermelon.

Dr. Day stuck his cigarette back in a bird's beak, soaked a cotton ball with alcohol, and swabbed the needle and then the side of my knee. He looked up. He'd acquired a permanent squint from all the cigarette smoke.

"Don't watch," he said. "Don't move your knee."

It seemed like good advice. I tried to concentrate on the brilliant blue October sky beyond the frosted-glass window. October is glorious in Illinois, cool and warm at the same time—the best weather of the year. The bus rides to away games took us through countryside where the last few farmers holding out against the suburbs still shocked corn in the fields. I tried to think about that for a while.

No good. I had to watch. I looked down past Dr. Day's fat rolls and bristly hair and the scaly red skin behind his meaty ears toward my knee. The needle approached. He pushed it in from the left front, sliding it in laterally, behind the kneecap, to a point where it went between the upper and lower leg bones, into the middle of everything. It hurt like a son of a bitch. It was the kind of pain that triggers that shocky light-headedness, the kind that makes your adrenaline surge. It was that "well, you sure as hell did it to yourself this time, didn't you?" kind of pain.

Satisfied with the way he had positioned the needle, he pulled the syringe plunger out slowly, and the barrel of the syringe filled with fluid the color of oxblood Shinola. He unscrewed the syringe and, pushing the plunger in, emptied the fluid into the stainless steel bowl. Except for the whistle and sough of his breathing, the room was quiet.

For some reason, I'd expected him to pull the entire needle out to empty the syringe. But there was the receptor end of the needle, still protruding from the side of my knee. He reattached the syringe, filled it again, detached it, emptied it, and reattached it again. And again. And again. And again. The last time, he pulled the needle out.

His cigarette, unattended for too long, had sagged its ash across the tray and smoldered out in the bird's beak. He fished the pack from his green rayon pocket and lit up.

"Get him some crutches," he told the nurse, squinting through the fresh column of smoke. She left on her errand, and he turned to my father, who was fumbling for a match for another smoke of his own. Dr. Day lit both cigarettes, and the two of them sat there.

"We'll watch it for a week or two," he said. "Might have to drain it again before it settles down."

"Pull your trousers up, Football Hero," my father said. "Let's go home."

Coach

It was a beautiful autumn afternoon—a Saturday in the year John F. Kennedy was killed. The marching band had just finished playing the national anthem, and now Coach was hobbling up the sideline, on those football-damaged knees of his, toward me. He was hot about something, and he grabbed the face mask on my helmet and started figure-eighting my head around—a classic old-time coach's way of getting a dullard's attention.

I remember being inside the helmet—the blue autumn sky and the stands and press box pitching and yawing crazily out there in the distance, and Coach's face, apoplectic, much closer. I remember, too, wondering what I might have done to trigger so much anger.

Coach came to the point. He didn't stop jerking my head back and forth, but he came to the point. It seems I had forgotten to remove my helmet during the national anthem.

He jerked a thumb over his shoulder at the flagpole careening in the distance. "Someday you'll know what that flag stands for," he yelled with the fervor of a true believer. It had been a completely innocent mistake, but he'd indicted and convicted me anyhow. I was from that moment and forever after an insolent young antipatriot beatnik, a rock-a-billy scofflaw communist rebel without a cause.

Coach had been too young for World War II and 4-F with those football knees when Korea heated up. He'd come from

64

the working class, and he'd put himself through college playing football, and he'd chosen to teach and coach. He was on top of his game when the school won the North Suburban Conference championship only three years before. But time was beginning to work against him. He could feel it. We all could. The plays in our playbook were archaic. The school district had spun off another high school and halved the student population. We were going up against schools three times our size.

Young people were changing, too. The year before, one of our captains eloped with his pregnant girlfriend. I had blown out a knee that season and got to rehab it in the training room whirlpool at lunchtime. The groom-to-be was there most afternoons, too, talking about how much he loved her and how they were going to go camping together over the summer. It sounded like bullshit to me, but it obviously happened. When the league found out we had a married man and father-to-be on the squad, we had to forfeit the few wins we'd eked out.

That had been the year before. This year wasn't much better. We just weren't a very good football team. In fact, we sucked. Week after week our losing ways continued, and as the losses mounted, our practices, always lackluster affairs, became even more dispirited. We sucked. God, we sucked.

On game days, Coach brought in the big phonograph from the music department and pumped the locker room full of college football fight songs sung by Mitch Miller and the Sing Along Gang. For two hours before we took the field, it was West Point's "On Brave Old Army Team" and Ohio State's "Across the Field" and Michigan's "Hail to the Victors" and Southern Cal's "Fight On." And on. And surreally on.

The music did little to lift the pregame pall. We sat in front of our lockers in silence, listening grimly, awash in a futile, smoldering, testosterone-filled hostility and black-hearted resentment. If we couldn't win—and to a man we didn't think we could—we could at least make things painful for our opponents. We could serve them up a big old shitburger of a game full of late hits and cheap shots and meaningless penalties. The going was about to get tough, and when the going got tough, we resorted to stupidity.

Ever the pure-hearted, straight-shooting believer, Coach tried to teach us to go out there and fight righteously. His brand of football was about sportsmanship and playing the game the way it was meant to be played. If we couldn't win, we could at least build character and make memories—character and memories that would serve us well for the rest of our lives.

When the chips were down and our backs were against the wall—which was pretty much every week—he brought in a nervous little man with a clipboard to deliver an inspirational speech before we took the field. The nervous little man had been student manager on Coach's college team, and he shared Coach's belief in God, America, and football. Week after week, he would look up at the ceiling. The fluorescent lights would glint off his glasses. He would take a deep breath, fix one or two of the guys with a righteous glare, and start his speech on an innocuously low-key and obvious point, something like, "Well boys, this is it. The Barrington game..."

Referring to his clipboard now and then, he would begin to build steam. He would recall every slight (real or imagined), every missed call, every Barrington cheap shot and lucky break, and every opportunity we'd fumbled away in the storied history of the rivalry.

He would pile bad break on top of unlucky bounce, injury on top of indignity, working himself slowly to a crescendo. He would pace and chew and jawbone and snarl and seethe and scrap and yap like a Jack Russell terrier on a rag doll, building a righteous, Elmer Gantry–like indignation.

Then suddenly, clipboard high overhead, he would pause in mid-rant, as if struck by some new and incredibly more important thought. The clipboard would come down. So, too, would the tone. Where only fifteen seconds before it had been ringing, now it was confidential, cajoling.

"I don't have to tell you this one's important, boys," he would wheedle. "This is Barrington, for goodness' sake. Bare...Ring... Ton..."

He would begin to build anew—a series of "I don't have to tell yous."

"I don't have to tell you how important this is..."

"I don't have to tell you how bad Coach wants this win..."

"I don't have to tell you the whole season is riding on this one..."

When he finished telling us everything he didn't have to tell us, he turned his attention to the memories we were making for ourselves. These were the best days we would ever know, so let's go out there and make the kind of memories we could be proud of in the future.

His voice always broke on the word "proud." This was our cue to stand and put our helmets on. He would use "proud" three or four more times—"Go out there and make your parents proud. Your school proud. Your town proud." If the game was big enough, he would even manage to make himself cry just a little, like an old Lakota medicine man coaxing a few raindrops out of a clear Black Hills sky.

And we would huddle up and lean in and give a big, albeit false-hearted, cheer. We would clatter out of the locker room on our high-topped football cleats, smelling of fresh athletic tape, pine tar, and a mentholated substance called Atomic Balm, and we would push down the hall and out into the brilliant autumn sunlight. We would stride across the parking lot and through the gates and take the football field—our football field—with a gritty but thinly rooted sense of purpose.

And we would lose. Week after week, we would fail Coach and our parents and our school and our town. We would send the nervous little man back to the well for more tears and more inspiration.

"Well, boys, this is it. The Crystal Lake game..."

"Well, boys, this is it. The Woodstock game..."

"Well, boys, this is it. The Zion game..."

I haven't seen a copy of the yearbook for forty years. I doubt there is any other place where I could confirm the team record. I don't need to. Our record is etched on my heart: 0–7–1. We battled to an uplifting 0–0 tie at homecoming—a moral victory that echoes down through the ages.

The season and daylight savings time ended the first week of November. Darkness cut practices short. That was all right. We didn't need practice. We knew how to lose, and after we lost that last game, we turned our equipment in and football season was over.

Thirteen days later, someone killed John Kennedy. It was a Friday. It rained that cold, steady November rain that strips the dead leaves from the trees. It rained like it was never going to stop.

Coach's America is gone. As gone as his T-formation offense and his Oklahoma 5-4 defense. The nervous little man is probably gone now, too—and maybe even Coach himself. Wherever he is, I hope he knows I know what that flag means now. The U.S. Army gave me a really good education on the subject. I always take my hat off for the national anthem, and when it's over, I crane my neck a couple of times to work out a couple of kinks—an old football injury—before I put it back on.

Leroy

I'm guessing Leroy (Luh-ROY, not LEE-roy) graduated from Libertyville High School in 1924, and he had worked in stores up and down Milwaukee Avenue in Libertyville ever since— the hardware store, grocery stores, the drugstore off and on for a while. When the IGA closed in the early fifties, he came back to the drugstore and worked full-time there—first for Mr. Taylor, then for Mr. Wilson.

He wore short-sleeved, bleach-yellowed, mostly synthetic dress shirts, bolo ties, those trousers guys who didn't wear suits used to wear to work every day, and comfortable shoes, really comfortable shoes. Leroy's arches had long since fallen. And ACE bandages for his various varicosities. On the job, he brought the entire ensemble together with one of the gray, crisply starched clerk's jackets that everyone who worked at Wilson's (but wasn't a pharmacist) wore. He set off the look with an ink-stained pocket protector full of ballpoint pens and grease pencils.

Leroy didn't have a written job description, and frankly, he didn't need one. After more than forty years of retail, he knew the ropes and stayed contentedly busy without supervision. He would get a little testy if the young pharmacist who had eyes on buying the place from Mr. Wilson decided to stick his nose in and supervise him.

He delivered prescriptions. He took deposits two doors down the block to the savings and loan and brought back rolls of coins for change. He swept and mopped the floors, stocked the shelves, straightened the magazine rack, and washed windows, waiting on customers the whole time. He checked incoming orders against invoices to make sure things toted up right. When business was slow, he would slip over to the feminine products counter and wrap the Kotex and Modess boxes in green paper and label them in grease pencil ("K" for Kotex, "M" for Modess) so we could all be discreet about that particular transaction when the time came.

Most important of all, Leroy maintained the drugstore soda fountain. Ancient Rome had the Forum. New York has Times Square. For more than fifty years, Libertyville had the soda fountain at the drugstore. Anyone who was anyone would drop by now and then. You might live in Libertyville, but you weren't from Libertyville if you weren't a regular at the soda fountain for the phosphates and sodas after school or for a sundae while you were out for a walk after supper. Or a malt or a shake or, on an especially harrowing business day, maybe a Bromo-Seltzer, hand-mixed by Leroy. He'd put the salts in one glass, pour another glass full of water over them, tumble the white foaming mix from glass to glass until it was fizzing properly, and set it in front of the stressed-out businessman who would toss it off in one big quaff, then wait for the belch we all knew was coming, which he would politely suppress.

Leroy was the lord of the soda fountain. He ordered the ice cream and syrups and polished the chrome. Once a month, he cooked up a big batch of chocolate sauce on the gas ring in the corner of the drugstore's backroom—cooked it up to his own taste and specifications.

Mr. Wilson may have owned the store, but Leroy asserted his own unique dominion over the high-ceilinged old space. It was all dark wood, tall shelves, and glass display cases, with a cigar counter from the days when cigars were cigars. The cash register sat on top of the cigar counter. The glass was scratched to near opacity by generations of coin transactions.

He had a space of his own—a fortress of solitude, where he could retreat for a moment and survey his fiefdom. It was just past the corner of the soda fountain, near the feminine hygiene products, almost out of sight, not quite in the backroom. He kept a small stamped-metal ashtray over there, and he kept a nonfiltered Kool Regular cigarette smoldering in it, two inches of ash sagging away from the Kool's ember. Every so often, he would pad over there on those ACE-bandaged legs and fallen arches. He would take a drag and, keeping an eye on the store, contemplate which of his hundreds of odd jobs to undertake next.

Everyone smoked hard back then, and not "lite" cigarettes. Marlboro Reds were as slack-wristed a smoke as you would want to be seen with. Real men smoked unfiltered brands like Lucky Strike, Camels, Old Gold Straights, Pall Malls, or Kool Regulars. So did a lot of real women.

Even by the standards of that day, a Kool Regular was one nasty little son of a bitch of a cigarette. It burned hot and harsh, and worse yet, it was mentholated. The Vicks VapoRub–flavored smoke all but blistered your windpipe on the way down.

The TV commercials said menthol was medicinal, that it was cooling and soothing and helped your smoker's cough. In fairness to the tobacco companies, there was a good chance your doctor smoked a mentholated brand himself. Although Leroy had the faintest hint of a smoker's cough—a kind of a dry, clear-your-throat-sounding thing—he wasn't smoking Kool Regulars for his health. He smoked Kool Regulars because no one, not even the worst nicotine addict, would bum a Kool Regular from him, not if there were anything else at all to smoke.

He could leave a pack of Kool Regulars by his ashtray and know with absolute certainty that young guys like me—part-time high school guys who routinely stole cigarettes from any unattended pack rather than buy them—would smoke cigarette butts we found in the family car ashtray rather than hook a Kool Regular.

So Leroy fiddled around the store while his Kool burned, doing an odd job, then padding back to his corner and taking a drag. He smoked like Bogart, holding the cigarette with his thumb and forefinger, cupping his hand and hiding the ember, keeping the cigarette hidden back there. It must have been a street-corner teenage tough-guy affectation when he started smoking—something he picked up from the movies or from one of the World War I guys who'd learned to cup their butts to keep the ember glow hidden in the trenches. Now it was just the way Leroy smoked—the way he had smoked for forty years. I can still see him, over there in his corner, looking out over his empire, one hand cupping his Kool, the other slid into the side pocket of his clerk's jacket. It was a pose worthy of a Fitzgerald dust jacket.

The store really was a town crossroads, and the job called for near-Victorian discretion. If Mr. Wilson or the young ambitious pharmacist wasn't available, male customers confided in Leroy. They would come in, wave him over to the side, and whisper something.

Then Leroy would disappear into the backroom and return with a three-pack of condoms secreted in one of the smallish, professional-looking white bags we used for prescription bottles. He became Leroy, Keeper of Confidences, Dispenser of Contraception. All I knew of sex was what I had read in a purloined copy of *Peyton Place* hidden in a textbook during study hall and a vague 16 mm movie the freshman football coach had shown the guys in health class. Leroy not only knew everything about the subject, Leroy knew how much sex people in town were having—and with whom. And that wasn't all that people confided in him about. Crabs to carbuncles, head lice to hemorrhoids, hair dye to athlete's foot, people confessed to him in hushed tones, and he gave them over-the-counter absolution. Ministers had the confidence of their congregations; Leroy had the confidence of the entire town, and I never heard him betray anyone.

He had the personality of an old sheltie—loyal and ingratiating to Mr. Wilson and tolerant (for the most part) of the young pharmacist. He would snap at young part-time help like me from time to time, and we weren't above poking him just to see what he might do.

He had an all-but-agoraphobic wife, whom he coaxed into going to the A&P now and then. They lived in a plain little house at the edge of town out where the sidewalks ended—a house with lackluster hydrangeas by the driveway and ratty overgrown yews under the picture window. When the word "nondescript" showed up on a tenth-grade vocabulary list, I remember thinking "Leroy's house."

When he worked days, he went home to have lunch with his wife. When he worked afternoons to closing, he went home to have supper with her. It was only five minutes away, and lunch or supper, his meal breaks were always one hour on the button. He'd leave in a hurry, looking hungry, and come sauntering back exactly sixty minutes later, all contentment, a toothpick in the corner of his mouth.

He was the first adult I came to know who had completely accepted his station in life. He was comfortable with its rhythms and routines, and if higher ambition ever wormed its way into his head, he'd made a separate peace with it long before I met him. There was a time to every purpose under heaven and in the drugstore: a time to stock, a time to sweep, a time to sell some soda fountain regular a new self-winding Timex from the rotating display case atop the gift counter. If Leroy aspired to anything at all, it might have been to live in even more perfect harmony with his town and his time, to mind his own business and be helpful, to foster a more pleasant commercial experience for Wilson's patrons. I'm not sure it would have been possible to do what Leroy did any better than Leroy did it.

Was it simplicity? Wisdom? Both? Had he achieved some

form of Methodist and Chamber of Commerce enlightenment? Was there some point where he'd said, "This is working for me. I'm all right with this"?

I was young, and youth would be served. During the twenty to thirty hours I worked each week, Leroy served me up reason after reason to scorn him. He was old. He was tired. He'd sold himself out. He shuffled. His back ached when he bent over to switch out the heavy rubber runner inside the front door. The list of Leroy's faults was endless, and he fueled a smug glibness in me. Like the Pharisee thanking God for being different from other men, I was grateful for being different from Leroy. I was destined to be someone. I was going to go out there and make something of myself. It was me all the time. Me, me, me.

Days came. Days went. Seasons flowed. Years passed. Eventually, I hung up my gray drugstore clerk's jacket for the last time, and ego arrayed in advance to announce my approach, I set out to conquer the world.

My understanding of life at the drugstore gets sketchy at this point. I know Mr. Wilson finally sold the store to the younger pharmacist, who moved it to a strip mall at the edge of town and added a big Hallmark-like gift section. The soda fountain was long gone by then, but the young pharmacist almost certainly would have taken Leroy along, fountain or not. The old sheltie would have switched loyalties somewhat irascibly, but he would have gotten it done all right. He would have provided a little reassuring hometown continuity during the transition—even if it meant having to step outside to take a few drags off a Kool Regular (the new owner was asthmatic and surely would have banned smoking in the store).

At some point a few years after the move, the two of them probably feathered his hours back. Maybe they let him just work daytime hours so he could be home at dark. No doubt the day came when he couldn't keep up and retired. No doubt Leroy is gone now.

As for my inflated sense of self, it has shrunk and wrinkled over the years—like an old helium balloon. It doesn't bounce against the ceiling any more. It has descended—first to face level and now even lower. I'm about the same age Leroy was back when I knew him, and my ego is floating at mid-shin height. As I write this, it's somewhere over there behind the arm of the sofa, where a draft from a furnace vent keeps it pinned in a corner.

Sometimes at night, the spirits of people with reason to resent my insufferable ego come to visit. They pass in procession—like Shakespearean ghosts—through the dim light at the foot of the bed.

Leroy is there, in his rightful place near the front of the line in his bleach-yellowed shirt and bolo tie, one hand in the pocket of his clerk's jacket, the other cupping a Kool Regular. I tell him I'm sorry about all the disrespect. He shrugs.

"It's all right," he says. "Go get the broom and sweep the front sidewalk."

Wrestling Eddie Dutzler

I was clicking through channels the other night, and I happened across one devoted to Big Ten sports. They were showing a wrestling match between the University of Iowa and the University of Illinois. A pair of corn-fed, land-grant heavyweights overflowed their singlets and circled and pawed at one another, looking for an opening, while their cauliflower-eared coaches, ill-fitting sport coats off, ties loosened, elbows on knees, yelled instructions from the bench.

I am not a wrestling fan and never have been. The NCAA could hold the national finals on my neighbor's front lawn, and I wouldn't bother to haul myself up off the sofa, cross the living room, and peek through the drapes. Sitting there the other night, watching those two young behemoths for a moment, I was drawn back to the beginning of my aversion to wrestling—to high school gym class where, every day for a couple of weeks in the dead of each winter, I had to wrestle Eddie Dutzler.

Dutzler was a big, quiet, gentle, not especially athletic kid with a head full of dark peasant hair that stood up on its own. We'd gone to school together for twelve years, and over all those years, I don't think I heard him volunteer ten sentences. He carried himself with a heavy, deliberate precision—with a comportment that was not so much above the rest of us as off to one side somehow. Eddie Dutzler was never near ground zero when classroom trouble struck.

He was an only child born to a devoutly Catholic older couple. As best I can remember, his father was a large, very quiet man who looked like he worked as an office clerk somewhere. Or maybe a loading dock supervisor. His mother was high-waisted and a bit on the heavy side. I can still see the three of them on their knees at Sunday mass, big-boned, ample fore and aft, an introverted family unit in the dim light of the tall old church.

Sitting there with my parents and my four brothers and four sisters, I used to wonder what life might have been like chez Dutzler—so quiet, so orderly. I envisioned the three of them eating dinner at the kitchen table, spooning their soup in—cabbage soup—without speaking a word. I imagined a pendulum clock tock-tocking on a wall in some other room. It was soup slurps and tocking, soup slurps and tocking, Mrs. Dutzler's canary in its cage in the living room having clocked off for the day at sunset. As I imagined it, Eddie Dutzler came by his taciturnity genetically.

He was always a nice enough guy. There just didn't seem to be a lot of whatever the stuff is that kids use to make friends with other kids. He was big, bordering on ponderous, and somehow it seemed like any friendship with Dutzler would have bordered on ponderous, too. From my interactions with Eddie on the playground and in class, I'd say he was smart but naively puritanical the way only children tend to be—the kind of kid who could help you solve for x but who would cover his eyes and go straight to confession if you showed him Miss March. It felt as if he were keeping the guys at arm's length for some reason. There was a gap there. That's all, just an unspoken gap.

There was no gap during gym class wrestling season. Not for me. Five days a week, two weeks every year, we would adjourn to the wrestling room, line up from smallest to largest and count off by twos. No matter how the counting went, year after year, it was Eddie Dutzler and me, always Eddie Dutzler and me.

The wrestling room was a windowless space, maybe forty by forty, with neoprene mats on the floor and a huge heater, suspended from the steel rafters overhead, with a massive blower pointing straight down. The way high school wrestling worked, they would crank up the heat in the wrestling room to help our gladiators lose weight before their next matches. If it was good enough for the wrestling team, it was good enough for gym class, and Coach would crank it up well over ninety degrees in there.

Both Dutzler and I weighed more than two hundred pounds by then, and we were not in the best physical condition. If we weren't sweating from the exertion of getting dressed for gym and walking down the hall to the wrestling room, the extra heat caused us both to break a sweat immediately upon arrival—and to continue to sweat profusely through gym class, the showers, and well into whatever our next classes may have been. We wore the same gym clothes every day without airing them. You started out clean and fresh on Monday. By midweek you were a bit damp and aromatic. By Friday you were a soggy, pungent wad. I see now that it was the smell of Eddie's sweaty wrestling room togs that led me to believe the Dutzlers had cabbage soup every night.

Neither Dutzler nor I was especially competitive. "You're a lover, not a fighter," the Old Man told me again and again, and he was right. Sometimes, when I meditate, I feel my way back through my genes, searching for any sign of a compulsion to dominate others. Except for a certain passive-aggressive streak, there is not much there. We are sneaky little people with delusions of grandeur.

Sometimes my father's father would strike a boxer's pose in front of the bathroom mirror while shaving. Standing there in his undershirt, he would throw a few jabs at his own image and say, "What I couldn't do to that Joe Louis." Then there was my mother's Uncle Bill, who once got even with a kid by pushing the kid's little sister into a ditch. Other than that, except for our few hapless stints of conscripted wartime service, the family tree is remarkably free of fighters.

At any rate, the entire class would be paired off, from the

ninety-pound, sand-in-the-face little guys, through the normal-sized adolescents, to the "good eaters" and glandular cases, to Eddie Dutzler and me, the two of us self-conscious and elephantine, in our place at our end of the mat. Coach would blow his whistle and one guy in each pair would assume the down position—on all fours. The other would take the up position, kneeling beside his man, one arm around the opponent's waist, the other hand on his elbow.

The object for the man on the bottom was to free himself from the upper man's grip—to escape. If you were on top, the object was to stay in control of your opponent—to break him down from all fours and to get him flat on the mat, at which point you could either ride him or go for a pin.

The case for revulsion was obvious. We were young men the approximate size and shape of manatees, young Catholic men not given to physical contact, and either up or down, the starting positions required physical contact. What's more, we were sweating profusely—from the roots of our hair and through our gym clothing. The sweat dripped into our eyes, down the tips of our noses, onto one another and onto the mat, which smelled of pimple cream and months of wrestling practice. Who knew what microbial evil was lurking in layers within that neoprene?

Then, too, there was the unfortunate eczema on Eddie's arms and legs—rashy, red, and flaking—an unhappy fact of Dutzler life around which I had to work gingerly. Rather than grab Dutzler firmly at the elbow, I would hold the joint delicately—like a really big teacup—between thumb and forefinger. Instead of pushing against him body to body, I would apply a gentle pressure at the hip and try to "suggest" he fall to his side—to lead him into submission as if this were a dance step down at Arthur Murray's, as if he were Ginger Rogers and I Fred Astaire.

And God bless Dutzler, he would follow. When he was in the down position, he would drop to his belly, roll to his back, and cease all resistance. It didn't take much of anything to get him

WRESTLING EDDIE DUTZLER   79

to say uncle. There were occasional awkward moments when he would try to fight back. But I had only to apply my forearm to the sweaty back of his head and bulldoze his face along the neoprene for a second and it would be over. It would be time to switch positions.

"Ready?" Coach would ask. Then he would blow his whistle and yell, "Wrestle."

Rather than drop to my belly, I would get to my feet awkwardly, like a man with two hundred pounds of dead weight clinging to his hips. Dutzler would hang on for a moment, then let me go. I would escape.

And so it would go. Up position. Down position. Ready? Wrestle. Again. Over and over. The scars are deep and permanent. I can't speak for Eddie, but high school gym class wrestling cauliflowered my soul. To this day, I can close my eyes and open my arms and feel Dutzler's man-child down-position girth. I can see his high-top sneakers, especially the ankle of the right one below and beyond the swell of his posterior, where I would grab him and lead him toward that flip to his back when the command to wrestle came. I can still sense that dull, doughy, adolescent pacifism. I can still smell cabbage soup.

Not our sport. Not how we would have chosen to spend fourth period. This was a cup that both Eddie Dutzler and I would just as soon have passed—another insulting fat-boy trauma to suppress.

"So how was school today?" I can hear Mother Dutzler asking at supper.

I sense the low, gentle thrum of Eddie's brain deciding how best to respond, Eddie toying with the cabbage, pushing it back and forth with the edge of his spoon. Should he tell her about our humiliation? Should he give her a glimpse into day-to-day life in the American adolescent male's world? Better to spare her. Why put her through it?

"Fine," I hear Dutzler telling his mother. "We had meatloaf for lunch. And sheet cake."

"Nice sheet cake?"

A shrug. Silence. Meatloaf and sheet cake and slurping and tocking.

I clicked away from the television wrestling match before anyone won or lost, before anyone had to assume the up or down position. I've been in this listless, low-grade ennui ever since. I'm in the down position. The thoughtless world is on top. When coach blows his whistle, it's going to take everything I can muster not to flip over and just give up.

Awkward Moment

My father wrote for the *Chicago Daily News* for more than thirty years, and he had a newspaperman's sense of writing style. It was who, what, where, when, and why, machine-gunned in short words, short sentences, and short paragraphs. Clarity, clarity, clarity was milled through a manual typewriter, marked up, and sent downstairs to the composition department via a system of pneumatic tubes that fascinated me as a child and seemed to go everywhere in the Daily News Building on West Madison Street.

I still have a copy of a memo to the staff that the hard-bitten, chain-smoking, alcoholic old city editor posted sometime in the early fifties in which he pleads for even more clarity and simplicity. He cites an old Chicago restaurateur who directed his kitchen help to "slice the meat thin. It'll never be tough."

My father gave the man what he asked for. He pared his writing down and punched it up until it read with the subtlety and the erratic staccato bump-clunk rhythms of a wire service teletype machine.

Call the style Chicago City Desk. It was great in its way— iconic and very pragmatic under pressure, when the rewrite desk was coming up on the third or fourth deadline of the day. There wasn't a news story in the world that was so complicated that it could withstand the battering power of the Chicago City Desk simple sentence. To this day, anytime a thought gets too unwieldy or a sentence starts springing leaks and blowing gaskets, I revert to Chicago City Desk. It torques everything down nice, tight, and fast.

But the style as my father practiced it stalled and balked around subtlety, coloration, and additional detail. When he wrote, he tended to send away anything that wasn't who, what, where, when, why, or how. What's more, like that of a lot of other newsmen, his version of the style seemed to treat the reader as if he or she weren't intelligent enough to figure the story out for him- or herself. With clarity came didacticism. It was the price of doing business.

My father stuck detail or color into his work when he wanted to evoke an emotional response in his reader. He was after a two-column-inch catharsis—a moment that touched the reader's heart and said something more by saying next to nothing at all. He wasn't always successful. Growing up reading his work every day, I quickly came to think his stabs at allusion too melodramatic. There was something overwrought in his understatements—they lay draped dramatically on the page like stone angels leaning on a tombstone and weeping.

The technique might have worked all right once in a while, but he went to that well all the time, it seemed. For me, lying on my belly, newspaper spread open on the living room floor, the trick got old fast. The melodrama and the implied disregard for the intelligence of his reader—those were the two big flaws.

He tended to grab you by the bridle rope and walk you from point to point. When he was on his game, there was a pleasant, personable pedantry afoot in his stuff. As the reader, you could draw any conclusion you liked, as long as it was his. When he was out of sorts, an alcoholic dudgeon would creep into his work. Like every other newsman back then, he went to bed drunk every night, and in order to bury the flaw and buffer the guilt, he appropriated an impossibly high moral ground—a fortress of rectitude from which he passed judgment, belabored points, led readers down paths, and then bludgeoned them with his outrage.

What outraged and upset him most was humanity's lack of compassion—peoples' amazing ability to ignore the pain and suffering of others. In Chicago (itself a gift that kept on giving stories to any half-awake newsman), the lack of compassion was everywhere. There was murder, political corruption, the mob, street crime, poverty, and race. One minute you were stepping over a dead wino frozen to the sidewalk. The next you were walking past a plate glass window full of people eating pastrami sandwiches and drinking beer. He was never without someone or something to be angry at or rail about when he was out of sorts.

I mention all this because, in telling the next story, part of me wants to channel my father, long dead now, no doubt having left the celestial city desk and ducked around the corner for a drink with the rest of the newsroom after putting the final edition of the day to bed. That part of me wants to lead you just far enough down the path to coldcock you with a moral that, by the time we get there, will be both glaringly obvious and inevitable.

But I can't work myself up to his kind of indignation, not even in Chicago City Desk style. Instead, I'll just tell the story.

Call him Mr. Schroeder. He taught at the high school for more than forty years. He lived in rented rooms a few blocks from school during the school year and disappeared during the summer. He was not married and never had been.

You got the idea that from mid-June until Labor Day he shared a beach house with some other aging bachelor, someplace classy like Cape Cod or the Hamptons. You could imagine the two of them sitting in Adirondack chairs, sipping something at cocktail hour, reading back issues of the *New Yorker* or maybe reading snippets of a Ford Madox Ford novel out loud to one another.

He wore well-made, sensible suits, the kind you went downtown on the North Shore Electric Railroad to buy at Marshal Field's, suits that wore well, lasted for years, and fit into a

84   AWKWARD MOMENT

weekly wardrobe rotation (if this is Tuesday, then I'll wear the charcoal gray).

His suits were a cut above anything else you'd see on the faculty. Middle-aged male teachers (World War II GI Bill types, alumni of Big Ten land-grant schools like Illinois or Iowa) wore cheap, Robert Hall suits. Younger male teachers, those who'd gone to college under the influence of rock and roll, later in the fifties and early sixties, wore sport coats. Coaches and shop teachers wore polo shirts. They—all of them—rumpled as the day went on. Not Mr. Schroeder. His suits looked as good when the final bell rang as they had when the first bell had rung that morning.

Forty years had given him that kindly old Mr. Chips aura. The next-most-senior teachers were young enough to have been his students. Everyone—teachers and staff alike—treated him in that too pleasant, condescending way people treat you when they think you're presenile or about to die of old age. There was a gap between Mr. Schroeder and the staff, and it grew a little wider with each passing year. There was an even bigger gap between Mr. Schroeder and his students.

He had been marginalized as he got older, forced away from his core in social studies and into teaching the courses at the edge of the curriculum—the benign, mandatory, tedious stuff the young and ambitious teachers didn't have time or temperament to teach.

He taught with a style from another era. He conducted class with a dignity that harkened back to a time when public secondary education was a privilege, not a place to kill time and wait for adulthood. He taught formally, very civilly, rhetorically, professorially. He worked from notes and lectured, pulling you up to his plane rather than descending to yours. I'm sure he'd learned the technique in teachers' college. Keeping students at a pleasant-yet-formal distance promoted order in the classroom and communicated a set of expectations. It dictated standards.

"If you have to raise your voice," you could almost hear his professor admonish him, "then you have already lost control of your classroom."

His techniques still worked, although just barely, on college-bound juniors and seniors. Times were changing. The first wave of baby boomers had arrived, and even the most adroit young teachers, trained and equipped with the latest techniques, were feeling the heat. Armed with little more than a chalkboard, a podium, and a book, Mr. Schroeder entered the classroom like a doddering old lion tamer, hoping to hang on to control for one more performance. The school administration did what it could to keep Mr. Schroeder from crossing the paths of young men who'd spent their high school careers in the shop wing or in courses like Introduction to Typing or Typing 2, 3, and 4. He was at his tenuous best with the college-bound kids.

By the time they were seniors, the denizens of the shop wing were emerging from adolescence into young adulthood. Most had jobs, some two or three jobs. They were more worldly than the college-bound crowd in many ways. It all came from working the kinds of jobs those of us who were going to college were forbidden to work.

The typing-class characters—you had to watch out for them. Neither college material nor possessed of mechanical aptitude, they were, by and large, killing time, waiting to graduate or to be permanently expelled—whichever came first.

One student, I will call him Jerry, was both a shop winger and a typing-class reprobate. Because the State of Illinois required all high school students to pass a course on the government of the State of Illinois in order to graduate, the administration had no choice but to assign him to Mr. Schroeder.

Jerry is not his real name, but he looked like a Jerry. He had red hair, and his ears stood out from the sides of his head. Two primal expressions took turns occupying his face: a malevolent, mischievous sneer and an "I'm gonna kick your ass" smile.

Second semester of senior year arrived. Spring seemed to come on forever. Bees buzzed in the lilacs outside the classroom windows, and Jerry, who was working nights as a mechanic in a truck stop somewhere by then, tended to cross his arms atop his pile of textbooks and catch up on his sleep during class.

Most teachers did not want to have their asses kicked. It was only a matter of weeks until Jerry concluded his formal education, so they applied a more contemporary teaching technique and let him doze. He needed his rest.

Mr. Schroeder, however, was old-fashioned. He was paid to teach, and so he taught. Always wearing his suit coat, never simply in shirtsleeves, he stood at his podium in front of the class, and looking down at his notes, droned on in drowsy concert with the bees. Whenever he discovered Jerry sleeping, he would stop and ask the young man a question about the government of Illinois. Nudged awake by a neighbor, Jerry would lift his head and shrug. Mr. Schroeder would answer his own question, Jerry would return to sleep. And so we would proceed, a day at a time, toward the end of the term and the end of high school.

One day in the third week of May, with only ten days of school left, Jerry was sleeping as usual. He had his grease-grubbed hands crossed atop his books and his head atop his hands.

"...and what do you think about that, Mr. Adams?" Mr. Schroeder asked Jerry.

Jerry raised his head and squinted. "Hunh?" he asked.

"The point I was just making concerning the governor's veto authority. What do you think of it?"

Jerry continued to squint for moment. Then he said, "Blow me," and put his head back down on his books. Mr. Schroeder was immediately flustered. He began fumbling with his notes.

"I...I beg your pardon?" he stammered.

Jerry lifted his head again, stared sleepily at the old man, and said, "Blow me...right now," Then he put his head down and went back to sleep. The typing-class males laughed and so did a handful of the college-bound boys. The girls didn't seem to have any reaction at all.

Flummoxed, Mr. Schroeder tried to collect himself and return to his lecture, but his mind was racing. His points came out in disjointed, mumbling spurts and half phrases. It was a terrible thing to have to witness, a terrible end to an earnest and humble career. Several awkward minutes later, the bell rang. Class ended and ten days later so did high school. Jerry joined the Marines that June. He pulled two tours in Vietnam and was awarded the Purple Heart. Mr. Schroeder retired and disappeared.

This is the point where, like my father, I am tempted to pick up my cudgel of compassion and start swinging. Then again, it might be better just to stop here and pose like a cemetery stone angel looking homeward.

Good-bye to Libertyville

It was a Saturday evening in early September, and my mother, my father, my buddy, and I were in the tan 1962 Chevrolet Biscayne nine-passenger station wagon driving to Glenview where I was to catch the overnight Milwaukee Road train to Minneapolis and college. A cousin of mine had tried college a year earlier, then opted to go into the air force instead. He'd given me his off-to-college trunk, and I'd packed it, taken it to the Railway Express office, and shipped it on ahead. The rest of my stuff was in an army surplus duffel bag riding between my buddy and me in the back of the station wagon.

It was a beautiful evening in the suburbs. One of those late summer cool fronts had come down out of the northwest—the kind that drops the temperature into the fifties for a night or two and makes it all but impossible not to think about autumn and going back to school.

Inside the station wagon, there was the faintest whiff of "don't let the door hit you in the ass" in the air. My parents had seven more children at home behind me. They needed the space I occupied—both physically and emotionally. Especially since I was their largest—I towered over them the way Li'l Abner towered over Mammy and Pappy Yokum. Now, lolling in the back seat, left elbow atop the duffel bag, smoking a Pall Mall (in front of them now that I was a college man), I had the strangest sense that maybe they weren't all that sorry to see me go. Were they gloating up there? Were they mourning the loss of a son or secretly celebrating shedding a two-hundred-twenty-pound obligation?

My parents were little, precise, proper people with impeccable manners. They paused before speaking and chose their words carefully. Their clothes fit them with Brooks Brothers perfection. They had furnished their home in a scale that fit them and surrounded themselves with books, magazines, and art that fit, too.

I, on the other hand, seemed to have my elbows on life's table. I hurtled between bouts of loud, often boorish behavior and stints of dark, adolescent moodiness. I instantly rumpled whatever clothing I fell into and had been too big for the living room furniture since eighth grade. At times, they seemed genuinely appalled to have spawned so large a churl. They had been horrified when, years ago, I'd brought home the buddy who was riding along to see me off to college—a large and even-more-oafish fellow traveler.

Like two astronauts in a space capsule going behind the moon, he and I had lost communication with the rest of the species as we entered our teens. The blackout phase had been long, dark, and isolating, and now I seemed to be coming out of it first. I had reestablished contact enough to be going to college. My buddy was staying home, continuing to clerk at the drugstore, waiting for something in life to enthrall him enough to warrant vocation.

So far, with the exception of underage alcohol, nothing really seemed to have caught his imagination. Wearing yesterday's clothes over yesterday's bleach-yellowed underwear, he wandered from a morning of work at the drugstore home to the afternoon Cubs games on WGN-TV and the Schlitz beer his parents had cached to drink with their coffee in the morning. Even I was concerned. The beer that made Milwaukee famous was making my buddy a listless lump. He was not even particularly interested in girls. He already had declared himself one of life's larger losers. He had abandoned all hope as he entered adulthood.

Two roads diverged in that tan Biscayne. Only four months earlier, weeks before graduation, he'd found a dead dogfish beside the lake behind the school during gym class. He'd smuggled it into study hall, and we'd had a fine time kicking it up and down the aisles. There had been all those summer and autumn evenings, wandering the quiet, tree-lined backstreets of Libertyville, smoking cigarettes, setting tin-can traps to unnerve passing motorists, looking for our signature brand of low-grade hell to raise. Now the friendship was fading. I looked at him across my duffel bag. Barely eighteen, he already looked middle-aged—paunchy, jowly, with glasses cocked up off his ears at a jaunty angle that, in those days, said "wise guy." There was only that faint, fading glow of mischief and juvenile delinquency to keep him from passing for thirty or more. The last cherry bomb was about to go off. We were twin louts in the backseat for the last time that evening. Even the waves of parental disapprobation seemed to have subsided. Why? Were they secretly smirking up there?

There wasn't much conversation that I can remember. The Old Man was one of those World War II autocrats who liked the car quiet when he drove. My mother can still ride for hours, staring out the side window, lost in her own thoughts, not saying a word. They were happy together in the car, holding small, elegant, perfectly proportioned hands.

We left Libertyville in pleasant enough silence. We took Saint Mary's Road south, crossing Highway 176 and the scar that was the old North Shore right of way, past new cul-de-sac subdivisions, past Adlai Stevenson's Kickapoo Farm, and out of Libertyville township. I should have turned and looked over the rear-facing third seat, out the rear window one more time. I would come back for the next couple of summers. I would sleep on the porch they'd converted into a bedroom. I would work at the drugstore one more year, then move on to a box factory and a sweltering summer job in a laundry. But I would never really get all the way back home to Libertyville. On school breaks and summer vacations, meeting people on Milwaukee Avenue, I sensed a growing distance. I would be from Libertyville—as much as a Chicago-born-moved-to-the-suburbs immigrant could be—but I would not be part of Libertyville anymore.

Lincolnshire came and went, Riverwoods and the rest of the suburbs, and then we were at the train station in Glenview. I bought a one-way coach ticket to Minneapolis, and after a few awkward moments on the platform, the train arrived. I shouldered my duffel bag and climbed aboard, and turning around, I looked down on the three of them, framed by the railroad car's vestibule steps and the door.

My parents looked like parents always look at train stations. Arms around one another, they did their best to hide their apprehension and look on the bright side. Or were they doing their best to hide the bright side and look apprehensive? I couldn't tell. Certain thoughts kept circling. They weren't losing a son. They were saving twenty-five dollars a week on the food bill. There would be more hot water for the rest of them. There would be that much less laundry for my mother to do...

My buddy stood smirking a kind of "so long, Numbnuts" goodbye behind them. Yeah, so long, Numbnuts. See you around.

The engineer started to throttle up. This was it. I waited for any final words of love or wisdom.

My father looked up, paused one last moment, and as the train lurched into motion he said, "Every day you stay in school will come as a severe shock to me."

Mademoiselle P.

She was a single woman in her sixties, a professor who had done graduate work at the Sorbonne back in her twenties. She had wandered through academia sans tenure since then, and now she was teaching remedial French to the churlish sons of second- and third-generation Irish and German Americans at a Benedictine men's college seventy-five miles north of Minneapolis. She was conjugating *être* again—this time in an austere classroom on the fourth floor of a dark old quadrangle late on Tuesday and Thursday afternoons, two and a half feet of snow in the bare oak woods and on the fallow cornfields rolling away to the west in the deepening, sunsetless twilight beyond the windows. I was one of the churls.

There were six of us. We sprawled, lolled, and slouched in the student desks in front of her. We exuded indolence, privilege, and a near-hostile reluctance to apply ourselves. We were big, young, strong, and male. Had we been cattle instead of humans, we would have been castrated and turned out to the feedlot by now. I'm sure she would not have objected.

We could smoke in class in those days, and a particularly acrid cigarette skank hung heavy in the classroom air, mixing with the smell of whatever it was they were cooking for supper in the refectory in the basement. The slightest hint of the scent of lilacs lingered near the front of the room, as if the ghost of Blanche DuBois had slunk by fifteen minutes ago. This we attributed to

93

the talc in Mademoiselle's pullet-like cleavage. We may have been wrong. The talc might have been chalk dust. The scent of lilacs might have been the last faint memory of some long-ago April evening in Paris hanging in mysterious wisps in the failing light of a late February afternoon in rural Minnesota.

We were, most of us, among the first in our families to go to college. As they had been doing for fifteen hundred years, the Benedictines were trying to infuse a classic education into us—no easy task in my case. History, philosophy, Latin, Greek, mathematics—all the stuff of a classic education was lost on me, as lost as the French subjunctive case would be were I ever to stumble across it in the fog of college sophomore *c'est moi* engulfing me. I was just sitting there, killing time, waiting for the five o'clock bell to ring in the quadrangle hall and the big bells on the church tower to follow. I was a clang and a mournful tolling away from escape.

There was a certain posture one adopted when killing time in those combination chair-desks. It involved leaning forward, left elbow on knee, right elbow atop papers on the desk's writing surface, cigarette smoldering between the fingers of the right hand. You stared at the floor, and jittered your right leg fitfully.

From the professor's platform, the pose must have communicated close-mindedness, a sense of futility, an unwillingness to even try to assimilate the material she offered. While I am sure I was enduring all of these, I am also sure I didn't intend to burden her with them. All these years later, I am sorry to have been so inconsiderate and disrespectful. It was rude, horribly rude.

Sometimes at night, when I review the long list of people I have offended over the years, I come to this woman, and I imagine her retreating from those classes, walking across the cold, dark campus, carrying her European satchel-style briefcase and the weight of her lonely world back to the wing of a residential hall she would have shared with a number of nun scholars who were there at the school to study something liturgical. I imagine a lover for her—a Frenchman—in Paris in one of those last summers before World War II. A Frenchman who disappeared in the underground. I see her sitting in the dayroom and reading Flaubert in French while the nuns nearby work and prattle about some abstract problem—transubstantiation, perhaps.

I let her memories of Paris color everything: Isle de la Cité, Pont Neuf. How quickly the Seine carried off their message in a *vin ordinaire* bottle. Everything.

I showed this to an old friend of mine—another failure at French. We met in her class.

"I am sitting in the front row next to you," he wrote all these years later. "This shared experience is the start of a great friendship. Good that we can look back now with sympathy and respect for her contribution to it."

Make the World Go Away

Vern, the warehouse foreman at the cardboard box factory, had artistic talent. He was forever drawing naked women in erotic poses on the massive rolls of paper that stood in the warehouse, waiting to be cut into sheets, printed, die-cut, folded, glued, and shipped. We would be gathered, three or four of us, leaning against one of the rolls—the box factory warehouseman's equivalent of leaning on a shovel. Vern would take a pencil from behind his ear and go to work. He had a gift, a real gift. The women he drew were Al Capp–like: leggy, languorous, recumbent, and seemingly receptive to the kind of advances that a gaggle of box factory warehousemen killing time between coffee breaks might stand around and fantasize about making. Vern should have answered that "Draw Me" ad from a matchbook cover.

"Huuunnnh?" he would say, stepping back from his latest masterpiece, seeking approval. He'd gesture toward it and kiss his fingertips. "Am I or am I not an artiste?"

The drawing would grace the warehouse for a day or two, then someone would clamp onto the roll and take it over to the sheeter. A pressman would slide the big axle through the core, hook it up, and start another run. Vern's masterpiece would begin her journey through the plant where she would disappear under the ink on some box for a hasp lock or elbow macaroni—whatever the line happened to be running that day. When I see one of those boxes, antique now, at a rummage sale or a flea market, I pick it up and

96

peer closely through my bifocals, down past the ink, looking for an ankle or a knee or a knowing half-smile, half-leer—or some other piece of female anatomy as drawn by Vern back there in the misogyny and heat of the box factory warehouse.

It was fiendishly hot that summer and humid the way only Chicago can be humid. In those days before emission control systems, the air was stagnant and stank of car exhaust, cigarettes, and red meat. Wherever you went, day or night, you could smell the concrete sweat. The routine stank, too. It was as if you were trapped—held in orbit by some nasty little work-sleep covalent bond. You worked your shift, you came home wrung out, you went to bed and lay there under an open window, listening to people on the night shift at the factories along the railroad spur work their shifts, the factory doors open to let in the cooler night air. Nebulous machines whirred. There was the occasional clang of some heavy piece of steel getting dropped. You fell asleep, and a minute later it was time to wake up and go back to the box factory and work your shift again. Clock onto the job. Work. Clock off. Sleep. Clock on. Work. Clock off. Sleep. Over and over through the heat of the Chicago summer.

When Vern had it in for you (which was all the time for me), he would tell you to go unload the boxcars of paper rolls on the railroad siding next to the warehouse. The rolls were packed in there so tightly that you had to open the boxcar door with a fork truck, then pick the load apart a roll at a time, shuttling each roll into the warehouse with the fork truck and stacking them twenty feet high. You eventually unloaded the car to the point where you could drive the fork truck onto the car and attack the load from inside. The car captured and held the heat of the day, and the fork truck exhaust came washing back over you. Had there been an OSHA, they would not have approved.

When you were on Vern's good side, he would tell you to hop on the fork truck and shunt pallets of sheeted paper stock out to the big Heidelberg printing presses on the air-conditioned factory floor. It was pleasant up there in the driver's seat. You could see the entire area, including the folding and hot-gluing line, where bored women—some old enough to be your grandmother, others young and sensuous enough to make cameo appearances in your over-heated midsummer night's dreams—tended tedious automated processes under the supervision of their own Vern, a fifty-year-old male with a forty-eight-inch waist, who ogled and groped his way through the shift like an inbred uncle at a family reunion.

As a member of the warehouse crew, driving a fork truck, you seemed exotic to the ladies of the folding and glue line. You were the wanderer. You roamed around the factory while they were stuck in the repetitive tedium of one place. Heads turned as you wheeled your load of paper down the main aisle toward the presses, as if you were a lone cowboy drifting into a one-horse town and they were schoolmarms or single women on the brink of spinsterhood.

"C'mon, Numbnuts, shake a leg," the pressman would yell over the roar of his machine. You would nod and smile knowingly for the ladies' benefit, as if he'd asked your opinion on some finer point of printing.

There were other characters out there on the floor. There was Harley, who spent his shift busting piles of die-cut boxes out of the pallet-stacked sheets of paper after they came off the presses. Exactly halfway from the start of the day to morning coffee break, Harley would adjourn to the bathroom for a ten-minute cigarette break. He would do the same halfway from lunch to the after-noon break. You could set your watch by Harley's habit.

There were the three brothers from Hazard, Kentucky, who worked with Harley—dangerous, hard-drinking, hippie-hating men who tried to shave me with a cheap stiletto on break one day. They lost interest when the knife proved too dull for the job.

There was a college kid named Tom, who knew the words to every song Elvis Presley ever recorded. Elvis was completely out of vogue by then, but Tom didn't care. Tom sang on anyhow.

"Find me a pink little poodle," he would sing as he pulled a hand truck of flat boxes to the beginning of the folding and hot-gluing line, "Lose my noodle over her...Chase her 'round all over town just to ruffle up her fur."

Some ladies would roll their eyes; others would roll their hips. The wide-bottomed foreman would come waddling toward Tom, an old rooster defending his hens. Tom would stack empty pallets on his hand truck and saunter off singing, "I'm a hunka burning love. A hunka, hunka burning love."

It was the era of the Hollies, the Young Rascals, Sam the Sham and the Pharaohs. The Beatles were big. The Rolling Stones couldn't get no satisfaction. Motown broke through with Smokey Robinson, Mary Wells, the Four Tops, and the Supremes. James Brown was saying it loud and saying it proud, although you didn't hear much of him around the box factory break room. The vast, postwar Appalachian diaspora—white southern hill people coming north to the city for work—was in evidence. You heard quite a bit of country music: David Houston singing "Almost Persuaded," Buck Owens singing "Tiger by the Tail," George Jones, Tammy Wynette, Marty Robbins, Eddy Arnold singing "Make the World Go Away."

"Make the world go away. Get it off of my shoulders. Say the things you used to say and make the world go away."

There, in the break room one afternoon, smoking a Camel and drinking a Coca-Cola, I saw the most promiscuous young woman on the folding and hot-gluing line poking a button on the sandwich vending machine, spinning the selection carousel, considering her alternatives, and singing loudly to no one in particular, "Make the world go away. Hang it over my shoulder..."

She was infinitely older than I was, maybe twenty-three, and she seemed to be joking and not joking at the same time. She seemed to be trolling for attention—for someone to talk to and flirt with. It could have been me, I thought. I could have walked over and helped her push that button, and who knows? Standing there, watching those stale sandwiches spin, maybe we could have made each other's worlds go away. In the heat of the summer, in the tedium of the box factory routine, I was tempted. Here was someone different and exotic and sultry the way certain women could be exotic and sultry if you happened to glance over and your hormones happened to be spiking at the moment. But that summer, a certain Catholic admonishment seemed to have annealed itself to my hormones—a "tsk, tsk, tsk" that ticked like a stopwatch and knew the most prurient part of my every prurient thought and kept me from acting in moments like this. So I sat and thought dirty thoughts, and the world went "tsk, tsk, tsk" until the bell rang and it was time to go back to work.

Clock on. Work. Clock off. Sleep. Clock on. Work. Clock off. Sleep. What wasn't monotony was misogyny and mixed messages from my hormones. What kind of world was this? My mother would drive me to work, and ten minutes later, there I would be with Vern and the warehouse crew, Vern gesturing toward his latest oeuvre and saying, "Huuunnnh?"

Vern transferred me to the swing shift in July—three to eleven. This was a different proposition entirely. When the front office went dark at five, the pace on the factory floor slowed. Even the big presses seemed to relax. An hour before quitting time, the night foreman would send somebody out for a case of beer, and we would split the shift into teams. One team tended the machines. The other went out to the parking lot and knocked back a beer or two. A few minutes later, the roles would reverse.

I'd been working the late shift for a couple of weeks when the female Eddy Arnold showed up, transferred too. Her reputation had preceded her, and all the men on the shift ogled. The bravest struck up bawdy conversations with her and helped her push the button on break. She loved it. The other women on the shift loathed her. But from afar, from across the break room, I sensed a change in her. She would go quiet when no one was looking, and a preoccupied look would appropriate her Kewpie doll face. Sometimes, she would sit and smoke alone.

The heat persisted. Two more weeks went by. Then one night, the warehouse night foreman told me to run a pallet of paper up to the presses. The factory floor was almost deserted when I drove out. There wasn't a guy in sight, except for the pressman. The folding and hot-gluing line was going, but the women were scowling and dour. Something was up.

"What's going on?" I shouted down to the pressman over the roar of his machine. I waved at the rest of the floor.

"She's knocked up," he yelled back. "Quitting...going home to Kentucky...saying good-bye to the guys out in the parking lot."

The last time I saw her, she was peeking back into the factory from an emergency exit door halfway down the south wall from the employees' entrance. I was on my fork truck, across the huge room, running yet another pallet of paper to the presses. She flashed a smile. "You?" I gave her a wave. "No thanks."

The next summer, I got a job driving a panel truck making pickups and dropoffs for a commercial laundry.

Screwed

It was a warm summer afternoon in 1966. I was standing at the counter in the Selective Service office in Waukegan with six or seven other young men. The local draft board was having its monthly meeting that afternoon, and we were all there to appeal our draft status.

It was a scene that played out over and over again in the tired old office building on Water Street. It was all a misunderstanding. The draft board had done us wrong. They didn't know who we were or what we were trying to achieve with our young and promising lives.

This was our chance to stand there and show them that we were worth more to society as young civilians than we would be as conscripts. And this was their chance to turn a deaf ear to this month's batch of cretins, to bring down that well-worn "Approved for Induction" stamp and yell "Next!"

My own misunderstanding with the draft board had begun on August 18 when they changed my classification from 2-S (draft-deferred college student) to 1-A (eligible for the draft). A paragon of bureaucratic efficiency, they'd immediately fired off a first-class form letter to let me know the good news.

Standing in my parents' kitchen after work on August 20, reading the letter, I knew exactly where the problem had begun. I had failed to take a test the prior spring—a national Selective Service test that would have proven I was making progress

102

toward a college degree. There may have been alcohol involved in my absenting myself from the test room that fateful Saturday morning. There may have been quite a bit of alcohol involved.

Like many other young men back then, I subscribed to a theory of personal exceptionalism. I thought myself too smart to be drafted or too good-looking or too something, I'm not sure what. The draft was for an inferior class of young men, not for a quick-witted young man en route to a meteoric career of some sort. I wasn't sure what the career would be in—English majors never are. But I was a young man in a hurry, and I had no time for the inconvenience induction into the armed services might cause.

Standing there in the kitchen, turning the problem over in my mind, I knew an appeal would be necessary. I considered an "I was drunk" defense.

Nah. The ranks of the U.S. Army, Navy, and Marine Corps teemed with young men who'd signed enlistment papers while drunk. The Air Force had a few, too. If all those guys sobered up and couldn't get out of their contracts, there was no way the draft board would accept drunkenness as an excuse in my case.

Slowly, plan B took shape. I would present them with letters from the president of my college and others attesting to my character and good standing as a student. That would show them. I would flank these with letters from solid citizens attesting to my status as a fine young man. I fired off a handful of requests. The college president and others responded, and now here I was, standing with all the other poor dumb shmoes in sport coats, waiting to be heard by the draft board.

The draft board office was on the second floor. You walked up a long, dark stairway, across a hall, through a Sam Spade–era frosted-glass door, and up to the counter. On the other side of the counter, the room was full of government file cabinets. Three prim, bored, menopausal women clerks sat at desks, pounding away on typewriters, completing forms and form letters, stuffing fate into no. 10 business envelopes, performing mindless ho-hum in-basket/out-basket stuff, pausing now and then to take drags off cigarettes and return them to government-issued aluminum ashtrays.

What must the office Christmas party have been like? Did they pull the dust covers over their IBM Selectrics a half hour early that day? Did they lock the door and break out a bottle of sherry and let the deferment and status change notices and orders to report for induction go unsent?

"Merry Christmas, Jan."

"Merry Christmas, Bunny, and Happy New Year. I just know '67 is going to be great for you."

There were several ominous piles of folders on the counter—our individual files that Jan and Bunny had pulled for today's hearings. The draft board itself was already in session in the conference room off to the right.

From the looks of the young men waiting to be heard, two types of cases would predominate the agenda. There were conscientious objectors—COs we called them—sensitive-looking, longer-haired men who were morally opposed to war in any form. And there were dolts like me who were morally opposed to giving the U.S. Army two years of our lives, one of which, if things followed the usual path, would be spent in Vietnam.

There was a certain *je ne sais quois* in the air—a general disapprobation. A massive, silent, almost fecal-smelling "harrumph" seemed to be radiating from the women, and it seemed to be aimed directly at us. We had our nerve, Jan and Bunny communicated to us telepathically. Whether we were COs or regular dolts, we were shirking our duty to God and country. If those women would have served on the draft board itself, not simply as civil service clerks, there wouldn't have been any of these hearing shenanigans. The bus to boot camp would be idling in the alley.

The hearings themselves were turning out to be perfunctory little affairs—five minutes tops. The conference room door would open; a man with a crushed look on his face would depart; the next man, looking as optimistic as possible, would straighten his tie, tug his sport coat sleeves into place, enter the conference room, and the door would close.

Sitting there, sheaf of letters in my lap, watching the draft board at work, I doubted my own exceptionalism for the first time. These people weren't screwing around. The members of the draft board didn't know the president of my university from Adam's off ox, or any of my other supporters for that matter. And from the looks on the faces of the men leaving the room, it didn't appear as if the draft board cared.

I was as alone as I had ever been. Not as alone as I would be soon, but pretty damned alone nonetheless. I could hear the "Approved for Induction" stamp fall: Bam! "Next!" Bam! "Next!" And then bam! I was next.

The conference room was wood paneled, with frosted-glass windows, something else out of a cheap film noire production. There was a long table with even more files strewn haphazardly atop it and those crappy brown coffee cups the government buys. And more of those cheap stamped-aluminum ashtrays overflowing with smoldering butts. The members had arranged themselves Last Supper–style along one side of the table, with the chairman in Jesus' spot. He was a big old boy in bib overalls—a construction worker, evidently. His hard hat sat on the radiator behind him. The rest of the board looked like Main Street businessmen.

My future was in the hands of the Rotary Club, Lake County's burgomasters, the kind of men who worked in their shops and offices all day, then dropped by the drugstore around four every afternoon to check the final stock market prices in the final edition of the afternoon paper. Pacific Gas and Electric preferred stockholders, World War II vets who might stop off at the Legion or the VFW for a beer and a bump on their way home to pot roast. Men with minds as monotonous as their middle-aged, avoirdupois-enveloped, missionary-position, twice-a-month suburban sex lives.

They had served. Through luck and gumption, they had survived. Now, twenty-one years later, they were still serving, sitting on the draft board, peering over the tops of their dime-store reading glasses at the next in an endless line of smart-asses parading past. Who did this guy think he was? What made him think he was better than the next sad sack with a sob story?

President Hard Hat picked up my file. He looked at it for a moment and handed it to a man on his right who looked like a chiropractor. He took a glimpse and handed it to a man on his right who looked like he owned a television repair shop.

"You had a deferment, son. You failed to demonstrate progress toward graduation from college. Why should we defer you further?" President Hard Hat asked.

"I was sick the day they gave the test." I kind of mumbled. Not a good way to start, but the game was clearly rigged. In truth, I had felt under the weather the morning of the test. Everything had still tasted like orange-flavored vodka. "And I *am* making progress toward graduation, sir. Here are letters from the president of my university and the chairman of the English department to prove it."

The letters followed my file up and down the table. In less than ninety seconds, my future was back, piled in a slovenly little heap in front of President Hard Hat. He glanced at the men to his left and right. No one said anything. They had seen all this before. President Hard Hat took off his reading glasses, closed his eyes, sighed, and pinched the bridge of his nose.

"I think we can safely say that unless you join ROTC you'll be in Vietnam a year from today."

He opened his eyes, put his glasses back on, and looked at me over the top of them. "Anything else?" he asked. "No?"

He inked up the rubber stamp and brought it down on my file. Bam.

"Next!"

I held the door for the next man, then turned. Jan and Bunny's mood seemed different now—slightly less judgmental, infinitely more smug. And why not? The U.S. Selective Service, for which they worked, had one more smart-assed college kid by the balls.

Joe

For a while, back in college, I tended bar in the small farm town near campus. There was a town bar, and there was a bar where the college crowd drank. I worked at the town bar, next door to the butcher and across the street from the Catholic church. It was the only church in town.

Hard-core regulars anchored the bar stools from the time we opened in the morning until suppertime. These were third-generation Stearns County Germans who'd grown up on farms and spoke English with a German accent. Hour after hour, day after day, they took turns buying rounds of tap beer for the house. It was a financial anomaly—a Grain Belt Ponzi scheme. If you bought a round, then everyone for whom you bought would buy you a beer in return, and somehow a few extra beers would come sliding your way as men came and went, buying their way in and out of the game. By noon, no one sitting at the bar knew who owed rounds to whom. We, the people behind the bar, were the only ones who tallied. We kept scraps of paper under the coin tray in the cash register and hash-marked down how many beers they'd bought. The customers were all on tabs.

These guys didn't work. They had bad backs or were laid off for the winter. It was something, always something. But they had huge farmers' hands—permanently calloused stacks of knuckles that looked to be eight or nine inches tall when they engulfed a beer glass or the dice cup. Their index fingers looked thick as broomsticks as they twirled them in the air—another round for the house.

Their wives worked—at the chicken processing plant mostly, performing the hard, dirty, unhappy jobs the rest of us never see or think about. They gutted. They plucked. They washed and packaged. On Friday nights, the women brought their paychecks to the bar, and the men had them endorse the checks. Then the men slid the checks across the bar to the man who owned the place, who settled their tabs and slid whatever was left of the check back across the bar to the men.

To celebrate this emancipation from debt, the men would point upward and rotate their index fingers—a round for the house. We would set everyone up, including all the wives, and start new tabs for the magnanimous sons of bitches. The cycle, having completed itself, would begin all over again—just like the cycles and rituals working their way through the calendar in the big stone church across the street.

The bar was a narrow, tall-ceilinged old space—a hole-in-the-wall on a gritty, gray street in a gritty, gray small town in winter. You opened the door and walked in and saw nothing but hunched backs and hams on bar stools, like so many hills in a landscape, rolling away toward the backdoor in a carcinogenic mist of cigarette smoke.

This was *Winesburg, Ohio* and *Our Town* without the callow yearning. These people had known one another their entire lives. They'd been born and raised right there. They'd married and intermarried across the street, and they'd tied a tight little genetic knot around themselves in the process. From my vaunted position on the service side of the bar, everyone was beginning to look just a little too much like they were related to everyone else. And everyone knew everyone else's story.

There was one old man, a favorite with the locals, Joe. He was well past eighty, a farmer who'd sold his place and moved his wife and himself into town.

"I sold eighty acres," Joe used to tell anyone who would listen. "I drank forty of that. I'm gonna drink the other forty, then you won't see old Joe no more."

He came and went by the alley door. Most mornings, he would shuffle in around nine-thirty, and he would stand at the bar in his long, threadbare overcoat, drink until noon, and then go home for lunch. After lunch, he would take a nap, then come back to the bar and drink until supper. Some nights, he'd come back after dinner.

He had blue eyes that seemed as merry as Santa Claus's at first. When you looked deeper, though, you could see something cold, hard, and blunt down there. Farming Stearns County in the first half of the twentieth century had not been a happy, elegant, or enlightening profession. When you looked in those eyes, you saw a brutal double helix wending and brooding through generations of peasant hardship back to the Dark Ages, where it disappeared into the Germanic tribal haze.

I never saw his wife. No one did. The man who owned the bar told me Joe had kept her alone out on the farm for decades. He said that in his day Joe had had a reputation as the meanest man in town. When Joe saw a big snowstorm coming in, he would hitch up his horses and drive into town to go on a drunk. He would leave his team hitched to his wagon, standing in the street outside the bar in the snow and the wind and the cold. Eventually, some local would take pity, unhitch them, lead them home, and stable them until the storm had blown through and Joe was ready to go home.

Those storms and his binges in town must have been a relief to his wife. With him gone to town, it would have been just her and the livestock and the chores and the storm. Sometimes I imagine her standing at the farmhouse kitchen window and watching him on the wagon, disappearing into the worsening weather. What peace she must have felt. I imagine her dread when, two days later, after the snow had stopped and the big cold

110　JOE

weather that always followed storms had set in, she looked out that same window and saw him coming back up the drive, leaving tracks in the new-fallen snow.

The locals treated him like a dear old uncle—a Teutonic Teddy Kennedy at their daily convention. He jollied them along. They liked it when he called me "you smart colletch kid" or "you young whippersnapper." They liked it when he announced he was leaving for lunch. "Blood soup, boys. She's making blood soup." They liked it when he held forth on his own mortality. "One of these days—you wait and see now—one of these days, old Joe will be gone." He was their buffoon, their comic relief, Falstaff and Lear and that foolish old professor that Marlene Dietrich reduced to nothing in *The Blue Angel*.

He was my buffoon, too. He was something tragic and comic and feeble and brutal, a cautionary tale concerning the ravages of alcohol, an unshaven, stupefied bundle of flaws and frailties standing in that worn overcoat, palms flat on the bar, partaking of all the free rounds, another beer and another shot always before him.

He's still my buffoon. I am not above taking him down and posing him in the corner of a short story or using him as an anecdote. I amuse people with stories about him at parties, or I promise myself I will write something important about him.

If not about him, then about his wife. I imagine her, old, living in town, washing the dishes after lunch as he naps on the horsehair sofa in the next room. I imagine the butcher knife— the same knife she'd used to cut fifty years of hogs' throats out on the farm—beneath the water at the bottom of the dishpan.

I use bits and pieces of Joe and his wife all the time. I've done it so much and for so long that I'm no longer sure where reality leaves off and fiction begins. Having been from outside, having stayed so briefly, I'm not sure how much of them I'm entitled to anymore—or if I was ever entitled to any of them in the first place. There's the real rub.

The man who owned the bar fired me late that winter. It

wasn't a friendly parting, and I took my custom around the corner to the college bar where I really belonged in the first place. I graduated that spring and lost touch with the locals completely.

My work takes me through the area sometimes. Interstate 94 sweeps just south and west of town, and I can see the road Joe and his team took. I look off to the west, past a rank of beautiful low hills, to see if maybe there's a storm coming in.

An Old Roommate Checks In

It's early morning in February. Sunrise is an hour and a half off. There's a full moon, and I'm shoveling four inches of new snow off the driveway. The thirteen-year-old, he of the strong, young back, is up there behind that dormer, sleeping the deep, rich sleep of adolescence. Somewhere out there in the dark, an owl is asking its perpetual question.

Shoveling snow became a form of contemplation for me decades ago. It's work to do while I wander the labyrinth of my existence, trying to move in God's general direction. The Benedictines have a saying: *ora et labora*. Pray and work. Give me new snow and a good shovel, and I'll buy that. It's simple, repetitive work. You make progress with every stroke, and you're free to tap into the holiness all around.

This morning, I think of a college roommate as I shovel—a man who grew up the only child of a divorced, dedicated, devoutly Catholic mother on his grandfather's dairy farm in Wisconsin. She wanted to give Holy Mother the Church a priest, but my roommate had other ideas. For a while, in our senior year and in the months after we'd graduated, when we were ROTC-commissioned second lieutenants waiting to go on active duty, we'd raised the kind of hell you raise when you're young and going to war and neither you nor society particularly cares one way or the other. What were the authorities going to do? Send us to Vietnam?

113

We drank. We drove fast. On Labor Day that year, we made the trip from Libertyville to Lake Street in Minneapolis—some three hundred and twenty miles through heavy traffic—in just under four hours. On another evening, up to no good, heading for the Twin Cities as fast as his car could take us, an open bottle of something in the car, we topped a hill and found a herd of Holsteins on the two-lane highway. They were too close to stop, so he steered and swerved through them. I can still see their serene faces just beyond the passenger-side window.

I was in love at the time, but he womanized enough for both of us. He had an eye for farm girls with healthy libidos who'd come to town to work in factories and drink in bars until closing time or the right man came along. Sometimes he tried to draw me into his schemes.

He called from a bar on the other side of the county around eleven on a very cold winter night. He was hot on some poor girl's trail, pursuing her with the relentless ardor of Pepé Le Pew. She had a roommate—right there at the bar, a mere twenty-five miles away. Her roommate, my roommate swore, wanted to meet me. She was dying to meet me, and she was beautiful. He thought she said she was a stewardess.

I did not want to go. My heart was spoken for. I'd met the girl of my dreams—the one I thought I would marry, the one with whom I would live happily ever after and make beautiful babies and take out a mortgage on a beautiful little house in the suburbs. Besides, even if I had been available, I knew his motive and didn't trust his judgment. Stewardesses did not hang out in working-men's bars at eleven at night when the temperature was below zero. He was persistent though, I'll give him that. I finally said, "What the hell," cleaned up, and drove over there.

He saw me and jumped out of the booth where the three of them were sitting the moment I walked in the door. If I didn't know better, I'd say he'd wanted to make sure I didn't have time to take in the situation and make an escape—if I'd had just half a second longer, I would have backed out the door and left. He gave me that "hey, old buddy of mine" routine from across the room. I trudged over, trying not to roll my eyes and sigh as I went.

His date was homely but obviously willing. She was draped on him like a fox stole on a rich widow at mass. She was bleary on seven-and-sevens and lust. My beautiful stewardess weighed at least two hundred and fifty pounds. She began with a beehive hairdo atop a huge head, and she spread out and down. She was a too-soft thing in a go-go dress and appeared to be wedged into the booth. It was all sag and belly under the table. There was not so much as the promise of a lap there.

I tried not to judge. I had long since become acutely aware I was not the second coming of James Dean. I counted myself a chivalrous guy, and trapped as I was, I sat down in what she had left of the booth and tried to be nice. I attempted to make conversation as we watched our respective roommates paw at one another and smile at us as if they were encouraging us to join in the fun. But the stewardess seemed to broadcast a preemptive, defensive hostility—the kind of hostility that women who've been told they're fat and ugly their whole lives emit when they come to truly believe they are fat and ugly. The bar itself didn't help her mood. It was a dark old working-class place—like the bar in *On the Waterfront*. Only this wasn't Eva Marie Saint. No, this was not Eva Marie Saint.

I plied her with small talk, and her responses came out in sullen grunts and snitty half sentences. She was not a stewardess. She was in beauty school. She had, however, done a stewardess's hair that day—hence my roommate's confusion. There was not much to say after that, and the two of us quickly lapsed into a buttressed silence and sat watching the show from the obviously happier pair across the booth. Soon that got old, and I excused myself and went to the men's room, where I decided to stay and wait for my roommate to come get me.

I lit and smoked a cigarette. I fiddled with the faucets and read the patent and manufacturing plate on the hot-air hand dryer. After a while, I smoked another cigarette. I cooled my heels another five minutes, and I was in the process of lighting a third cigarette when my roommate came in and asked what was wrong.

I explained my predicament. There was my long-standing relationship with my true love—a young woman whom he knew well. There were the stewardess's self-esteem and hostility issues. The beehive and go-go dress had me spooked. I was not then, nor am I now, the most spiritually graceful of men, so I may have pointed out her avoirdupois. I was a large young man in those days—the size of a college linebacker, anyhow. While she was not that tall, the stewardess weighed as much as a college offensive tackle. There was also the issue of my roommate having drawn me into the predicament. Friends didn't do that to friends—but he was in the throes of whatever you call these kinds of things, and he was slightly drunk. I would deal with that situation later.

It was a simple case of "Sorry, pal. No can do." After a few minutes of moping (no date for the stewardess meant no nothing for my roommate), he came around to my point of view. We gave the girls a ride home in his VW bug. The happy couple sat up front, the stewardess and I in the back, her side of the car riding slightly lower than mine.

What can I say? We were young and exuberant, and thanks to our upcoming stints with the U.S. Army, we had taken up residence at the corner of "who cares" and "not me." So many vices, so little time. Even alcoholism was new to us. I remember a period of time where we drank only ice-cream drinks—grasshoppers made with crème de menthe and something called a Scotch Ice House, a mix of vanilla ice cream, milk, and cheap Scotch.

Meanwhile, back home, his mother was praying for him, writing long letters to remind him he had come to her with a lily-white soul and urging him not to do anything to stain it. She pleaded for him to go to confession and to receive Holy Communion regularly. We could feel her over there in Wisconsin at night, on her knees beside her bed, tugging at the hem of God's robe, interceding on behalf of her boy.

No good. We were useless and Vietnam bound. We were sowing wild oats and marking time. And that fall, some time after the great Labor Day run from Libertyville to Lake Street, he went on active duty in the artillery. I reported for duty with the Signal Corps in January.

It was that thing with his mother, her wanting him to be a priest, I think, that made him volunteer for duty as a forward observer with the army of the Republic of Vietnam. Being a forward observer for the American artillery was dangerous. Being a forward observer for the South Vietnamese was much more so. That's what he was doing when we lost touch.

My own tour of duty in Vietnam was relatively uneventful. I brought home a sense that I was an outsider—that I didn't belong among people who hadn't gone to the war. Two and a half years as draft bait and two and a half years of active duty will do that to you.

Thirty years came and went, and I never heard from him. Then one day last fall, out of nowhere, he pinged in via e-mail. I recognized his cool, wry, almost formal tone right away, and we went back and forth, catching up, comparing notes on the war. He had seen a lot of combat and death and come home an outsider too. It was good to be back in touch.

There was no word from him over the holidays, and when I didn't hear from him by late January, I gave him an e-mail nudge. The damn holidays. Had they been as bad for him as they always are for me?

No response. I nudged again. Then late yesterday evening, he checked in. I was right. The holidays had been hard. He would write more when he got it together.

Ora et labora. It's still snowing, and that damned owl keeps asking its one damned question.

A Preinduction Reverie

Something about sitting in your underwear on a cold metal folding chair in the basement of the main post office in downtown Minneapolis before dawn in January, holding your preinduction physical paperwork, waiting for the clerks and doctors to start work, kind of deflates a guy. You're cold and virtually naked. The guy next to you is sporting an interesting rash. The guy in front of you should have gotten new underwear for Christmas. There's nothing to read, and if you pass the physical (why wouldn't you? you're twenty and in perfect health) the army will have your ass for two years. Not your day.

It's below zero outside, but what with the road salt and God-only-knows what else, the gutters run with a thick slurry of brown-black snow water. The doctors and clerks track it in and stomp their feet, leaving cold puddles where you and the rest of the day's lucky bastards will be standing barefoot soon. Not that the doctors and clerks are eager to begin. Far from it. The clock says they have five minutes before the workday begins—five minutes to sit at their desks, drink coffee, smoke cigarettes, and talk about last night in their everyday lives.

Somebody bowled a 193 at Nokomis Lanes. Somebody's girlfriend was pissed off about boys' night out. Somebody's wife wanted him to buy a house in Bloomington.

Meanwhile, over here, in your underwear on the folding chairs, somebody is about to get drafted. You are their morning's

118

in-box, the subhuman speed bump between them and lunch, the predawn pain in the ass. They look you over and size you up. Just how much of a pain in the ass will you be?

The second hand sweeps past twelve. Seven a.m. has arrived. The clerks stub out their cigarettes, take the dustcovers off their typewriters, and start pushing paper. An already bored young sergeant of some sort comes over, points to a grid of yellow tape beneath the slush puddles on the floor, and tells the group to line up along both sides of it and face the middle. C'mon, ladies. Let's go, let's go.

A doctor appears. Not much of a doctor, but a doctor nonetheless. He seems to be hemorrhaging failure. All that time in med school, an internship, a residency, and this is the best he can do. He thought he would cure cancer, but here he is, starting another day of induction physicals in the basement of the main post office in Minneapolis at seven in the morning. He tells the group to turn away from the center of the grid, drop its shorts, bend over, and spread its cheeks. There is resentment and hostility in his voice—as if the group had a hand in his underachievement; as if the group chose to get up before dawn, come down here, and inconvenience him by reporting as ordered; as if standing there in the cold, bent at the waist, underwear knotted around its slightly splayed knees, and spreading its cheeks made the group happy.

Dr. Depressed dons a latex finger cot and peers, pokes, and prods his way along the line, eventually getting around to telling the group to stand up and pull up its shorts. The group stands up and salvages what little dignity and modesty it can by pulling up its shorts. He tells it to turn around and face the center. The group turns around and faces the center. One man at a time, he examines the group for hernias, then sends us off on an odyssey along a green line on the floor and through a door, as if he were sending us into the Tunnel of Love. Only there's no love here. Bored, angry army medics await, staffing stations for blood pressure and hearing tests, demanding you pee in a cup. Eventually, the green line leads you to a clerk who is every bit as bored, angry, and hostile as the doctor and medics. The clerk takes your paperwork, mills it through his typewriter, stamps it a few times, and sends you back to sit on the cold folding chair in your underwear some more. You try to return to the folding chair on which you'd been sitting when all the fun started, but all the chairs are occupied except for the one where the guy with the rash had been sitting. You decide to stand. An angry clerk looks over and yells, "Hey! Numbnuts! Sit down!"

Doctor Depressed returns. Anything else the government should know about? Any preexisting conditions that might bar you from service?

You raise your hand and produce a note from the family doctor. It's that old football knee. You sure would like to go into the army, but . . . The doctor snatches the note, looks at it, and sends you to another hostile clerk, who stamps it up good, makes a phone call, and sends you to a specialist ten blocks away.

The specialist has a posh office on the ninth floor of a medical arts building, but he's every bit as bored, angry, and hostile as the clerks, medics, and doctor in the post office basement. He looks at the note and tells you to drop your pants and get up on the examining table. He takes out a tape measure. The bad knee is nearly two inches bigger around than the good one. He tells you to lie back. He picks up your leg and manipulates the joint. Mmmm. Nice and loose. It clicks and wobbles as if on cue. He tells you to duckwalk around, then checks the knee again and finds it to be even clickier and wobblier. He tells you to put your pants back on, and he sits there and thinks for a moment.

"You're a lucky man," he says.

"You mean . . ." you start to say, "you mean . . ."

Beyond his window a single ray of light pierces the clouds and seems to fall on the area of the city where the main post office sits. The Almighty is reaching down, touching your file, righting the terrible wrong your country had almost done you, staying Fate's hand. A halo of hope enters the room—and your heart.

"Yes. You'll have to have that operated on someday." He takes a big stamp and inks it up good on a pad. Why do these people always have stamps? "But for now it's fine. You passed the physical. You can serve."

He brings the stamp down on your form with suspiciously smug authority.

Dear John

There was a certain smell to army canvas, a heavy, tarpy, water-proofed funk. The S-4 supply section warehouse smelled of it. So did all the tents and cots when the battalion went into the field and jeeps with their tops up and the covered beds of the bigger trucks. Anywhere you went in the army, you could almost taste the canvas.

I was sitting by myself in the back end of a two-and-a-half-ton truck parked in the back row of the battalion motor pool in Germany, awash in the smell of canvas. I was about to open a letter from a certain young woman back home, and the back of the deuce and a half afforded me a little privacy—privacy I expected I was going to need.

The envelope was flimsy, frilly, and blue—the kind of young women's stationery they sold in flat boxes in drugstores, stationery for writing casual, happy, newsy little notes to a young man while he was away. But this note was not going to be casual or happy.

Her handwriting, in nineteen-cent blue ballpoint, was young and not especially graceful. Her initial capitals looked like a high school girl's, and the rest of her script appeared to be hung up halfway between high school and adulthood—like the tray full of nail polishes and drugstore perfume bottles on top of the dresser in her bedroom at her parents' house. The letter looked young and Midwestern adolescent feminine, and I sat there finding fault with it for a long time.

If you were going to write a goddamned Dear John letter, at least write it in an elegant hand. I wanted something you might expect from an F. Scott Fitzgerald heroine—something in fountain pen, something that looked like it had been written thoughtfully at a desk in the lobby of the Ritz in the failing afternoon light—not this.

This hadn't come from the Ritz. It had come from a big old house—the front half of a duplex she shared with four other young women near the University of Minnesota in Minneapolis. From the corner bedroom on the right at the top of the wide stairs, I suspected. Sitting there in the deuce and a half, I could all but hear the party going on downstairs in the living room in Minneapolis, the laughter and the music—the soundtrack from *Woodstock*—floating up as she wrote.

I could name everyone down there waiting for her to finish her painful little duty and come down and join them. They had been our friends. They were still hers. Since the army had taken me out of circulation, I wasn't relevant to them anymore. I was the gnu at the edge of the herd that the hyenas picked off and ate last week—a bleached skull and a few well-gnawed bones under hoof in the grass. Gone and forgotten.

I had said my good-byes to them, closed the door, and taken a cab to the airport. An awkward moment of silence may have hung there in my wake, but then someone reached over and turned up the stereo, and the party picked up steam again.

Luckily, the army provided me with new friends, a whole crowd of them. We were young officers assigned to a backwater outfit in Germany until it was time to go to Vietnam. Every night we would crowd along an officer's club bar where, only twenty-five years earlier, young Nazi officers had stood. We were so many latter-day poor little lambs, another lost generation drinking hard, feeling as hapless and helpless as the Nazis who'd preceded us must have felt.

We indulged ourselves. We had fast cars and motorcycles and money to spend. There were women—aging army schoolteachers and civilian employees and local German women smitten with Americans. Some nights, after the bar closed, the party would go from the officer's club bar back to the bachelor officers' quarters and continue until dawn. This was desperate, empty-headed, alcoholic-fueled hedonism at its finest. Waiting to go to war will do that to you.

I looked at the blue envelope again. A little more than a year before, I'd proposed to her. The army had my number, and I sensed the hyenas skulking in the tall grass. I wanted to tether myself to her—to something permanent and beautiful and meaningful. No matter what happened, I wanted to have us to come home to. So, on a beautiful September day, waiting for the bus on the corner of Twenty-Sixth Street and Bloomington Avenue in South Minneapolis, I proposed. She said yes. The bus came. Life proceeded, happily at first. Then something tentative crept in—a never-spoken hesitancy on her part that hung around and got heavier. Christmas and New Year's came and went feeling ominous. By the time I went on active duty in January, the relationship had picked up the cold damp sog of a Fort Gordon bivouac in a January drizzle.

God knows she tried to be newsy and cheerful on that blue drugstore stationery at first. And I tried to keep my letters light as well. So much was omitted. So much was lost in translation. On Sunday nights, when the long-distance rates were low, I would stand at a pay phone under a streetlight and feed dollar after dollar in quarters into the slot, buying three more minutes in which neither one of us really had much to say. She came to see me in May. I was stationed at Fort Monmouth in New Jersey then, and I remember her sitting close to me, again not saying much, as I drove her back to the airport in Newark for her trip home. And I managed a week of leave before shipping out for Germany that June.

I was a dead gnu. I didn't quite realize it, not even when she introduced me to a guy who lived in the back half of her duplex with four of his buddies. The whole leave was painful and raw and jagged, and I spent my last night with her in the bedroom at the top of those stairs, watching her sleep in my arms.

She worked at seven, and we said one of those awful good-byes before dawn. I was to fly out around noon, but at the airport I changed flights so I could go back and see her once more. I was there by the time clock when she clocked off.

When she saw me, she cried, and not happy tears. I should have stayed gone the first time. We said another awful good-bye, and I caught the plane with seconds to spare. The woman sitting next to me was drunk on Manhattans, and she smoked and vomited bagful after acrid bagful all the way to Chicago.

In the back of the deuce and a half in the back of the motor pool, I eventually opened the letter. It was two pages of the regular Dear John stuff, not especially deep and for damned sure not elegant. Then again, we hadn't been an especially deep or elegant couple. She ended it, "Hope you understand."

There are recurring themes and subliminal melodies in life—personal leitmotifs you can't help but pick up on eventually. They play softly and subtly at first but pick up amplitude and definition and insistence over time, and eventually life starts to hit you over the head with them.

Sitting there, rereading the letter, I sensed a theme—a recurring, less than subtle, not quite melody—taking form. I wish I could say it was fraught with romanticism, that it sounded like some overwrought piano piece by Schumann or Grieg. It didn't. It was two notes and probably better suited for the tuba than the piano.

"Not you," it said over and over. "Not you. Not you."

Not me. I wouldn't be marrying my college sweetheart and buying a house in the suburbs. No nine-to-five job, no Saturday afternoon barbeques with our friends on the patio, no standing there, flipping steaks, sipping longneck beers with the men, exchanging stock tips. Not me. Not me.

And while I was free now to grab all the hedonistic gusto I wanted, to live fast, drink, and womanize from the time the flag went down the pole in the evening until reveille the next morning, that was not me either. It began to rain. The gray German afternoon smelled like wet army canvas.

"Not you," sang the tuba. "Not you. Not you."

The Major

The battalion motor pool was a sheet-metal lean-to with an office attached to the north side of the structure. It sat on a sand beach on the bay side of the Cam Ranh peninsula, fenced in with triple-stacked concertina barbed wire, a two-man foxhole bunker facing the water, the gate on the north side. Driving in or out, the men in the big trucks had to drop them into six-wheel drive in order to get through the heavy sand dunes.

Those of us assigned to the motor pool shared the space with a colony of big lizards—three-, four-, and five-foot animals that lived in the low scrub on the dunes to the east behind the building. They were there, sunning themselves, warming up for the day, when we came to work in the morning. They were still there twelve hours later, catching the last of the setting sun's heat, when we left at night. Their tracks were everywhere in the sand and distinctive, their fore and rear feet working opposite/diagonal on primitive shoulders and hips, their heavy tails carving deep furrows, their tracks running this way and that.

"Fuck you," they would call with a distinctive, guttural grunt from the scrub behind the building. "Fuck you. Fuck you." A reptilian Vietnamese Greek chorus to remind me I was the battalion motor officer. I signed for every truck and tool. The men of the motor pool were my responsibility, too. This superheated, greasy empire was mine. All mine. Fuck me.

127

The Quonset hut battalion headquarters was in the sand too, across a crumbling tar road from the motor pool, a rundown, dilapidated little place as war weary as we were. You walked in and there were two or three clerks' desks and the sergeant major's desk and the adjutant's desk. The adjutant was a captain, the colonel's aide.

Their window air-conditioning unit was forever icing up and shutting down. The sergeant major and one of the clerks were always pulling the damned thing out of the wall to tinker with it. At least they had air-conditioning. The motor pool was all sheet metal and direct sunlight. I lost thirty pounds working there.

Behind the clerks, the sergeant major, and the adjutant, the major's office spanned the width of the headquarters building. You had to walk through it to get to the colonel's office at the back. The major was the battalion executive officer, second in command. His desk was on one side of the throughway to the colonel, and his sofa and file cabinet were on the other. Someone—the adjutant, a clerk, a company commander, a staff officer, the sergeant major—someone—was forever walking through the major's office. He may as well have had a desk on the 4 Train to Brooklyn, with people sliding through from car to car.

The major was a neat little man, crisp, quick, and assertive—even in the subtropical heat. When he came over to inspect the motor pool, he carried himself with a bandy swagger—even in the heavy sand. It was almost, but not quite, a strut, his elbows ever so slightly out, his head up, perpetually surveying the situation, asking questions, pointing things out. He was the quintessential U.S. Army officer. He was what the army trained you to be.

He was also ancient by my standards, probably all of thirty-five, and a sophisticate. He got the *New Yorker* at mail call, if I remember correctly, and *Harper's* and the *Atlantic*—hardly typical fare among army officers. He'd come to Vietnam from embassy duty in Argentina, where he'd acquired a fiancée, and he found time every afternoon to sit at his desk beside the stream of traffic to and from the colonel and, mood softer, write to her in Spanish.

He had mastered the art of splitting the difference between the cold formality that comes with rank and an overly friendly, one-of-the-guys informality to which weaker, less effective officers resorted. He befriended you and kept you at arm's length at the same time.

A savvy executive explained it to me once. "If you're a nice guy all the time and then one day you come down on somebody, everybody says, 'that no good son of a bitch.' But if you're a son of a bitch most of the time and do something nice once in a while, they say, 'Aw, look at that. He's a nice guy after all.'"

The major walked the tightrope between nice guy and son of a bitch gracefully. He was far too much of a soldier to discuss politics with subordinates. Somehow, though, when it came to the war, I could sense where he stood. He stood where he had to in order to continue to advance his career. He believed Vietnam was a noble undertaking. We had been sent there for a purpose. When we accomplished that purpose, we would be brought home with honor. Until then, he would conduct himself with unrelenting dedication and tenacious professionalism. He would demand as much from the officers serving under him, even if unrelenting dedication and tenacious professionalism were in short supply. By that point in the war, they were.

Richard Nixon had begun putting his "secret plan to end the war" into motion, and the plan called for turning many of the support functions that outfits like ours performed over to units of the army of South Vietnam. Our orders had changed. Now we were to support the South Vietnamese Army in every possible way. We fixed their equipment. We fixed their mistakes. We stepped in and did their job in its entirety whenever they dropped the ball, and they dropped the ball daily.

They were a never-ending assault on our sense of occidental superiority. We had arrived as the near-colonial masters. Now we had become the servants. We'd been drafted, trained, and shipped over here; we'd been deprived of the comforts of home, our lives on hold while the lives of our civilian peers went on comfortably uninterrupted. We found ourselves standing in the sweltering motor pool sand while a young Vietnamese truck driver, three months removed from a rice paddy, kicked a flat tire down from the bed of the two-and-a-half-ton truck the taxpayers of the United States had provided him and said, "You fix! Now!"

Grumbling, muttering, chafing, my men fixed. "Fuck you," croaked the lizards. "Fuck you. Fuck you."

There were other problems. Heroin was two dollars a fix, smuggled in by the mamasans who cleaned the company compound, washed clothes, and burned off barrels of latrine waste every morning. The enlisted men's billets smelled of Thai stick. The noncommissioned officer's area smelled of Jack Daniels.

There were wives back home cheating, and husbands cheating over here. There was venereal disease. There were medics who spent their entire tours shooting hypodermics of the latest wonder drugs into government-issued asses, where the drugs would do battle with increasingly bellicose strains of gonorrhea. There were weevils baked into the bread, rats under the latrine seats, and the unrelenting monotony of the twelve-on, twelve-off grind.

Meanwhile, in Paris, Henry Kissinger and the North Vietnamese had been arguing for months over the shape of the table around which they would begin to hold peace talks. "We gotta get out of this place," skinny girls in miniskirts fronting Pilipino bar bands sang in broken English in the service clubs every night, "if it's the last thing we ever do. "

Undaunted, the major soldiered on. He would waylay you as you left the colonel's office and press you for details concerning your men and everything else. What was the status of the thus-and-such report? Had Sergeant So-and-So heard anything more from his wife back home? Had you talked to Specialist Such-and-Such about reenlisting? How many trucks were available for that convoy to Nha Trang tomorrow? Had you completed the

Headquarters Company ammunition inventory yet? Was Lieutenant So-and-So coming down from Dalat on the morning chopper? His minutiae became your minutiae. He was the quintessential officer, the tenacious professional. Shoulder to the wheel, he pushed, dragged, wheedled, and led you and the rest of the battalion forward one day at a time.

He and the Sergeant Major maintained an additional duty roster—a list of junior officers available to take on the extra jobs, details, reports, investigations, and responsibilities that constantly came down from the First Signal Brigade in Saigon or, above the brigade, the U.S. Army Vietnam. When your name rose to the top, the major assigned the next additional duty to you. You dropped back to the bottom and went to work on the assignment, only to rise up the list again and again. Yours was not to reason why; yours was to get the assignment done and take on the next, always with that tenacious professionalism.

The worst additional duties were line of duty investigations. Whenever a GI got killed, wounded, or otherwise involved in an incident, the army required an officer to look into the matter and file a report. Was the soldier following standard operating procedures, orders, and regulations at the time of the incident? Had he or someone else broken the law somehow?

These were usually routine black-and-white assignments, but they could carry terrible responsibility. If you found the soldier to have acted outside the line of duty, he could be charged with a crime and court-martialed. He (or his survivors if he'd died) could be denied compensation or benefits. It was important stuff. You investigated as best you could. You gathered military police and hospital reports, interviewed witnesses, and eventually, inexorably, the facts found their way into the spaces on the forms. Subtleties, extenuating circumstances, and shades of gray fell away. Lives changed, not always for the better. In the process, your sense of tenacious professionalism got heavily taxed.

Here we were, young men who would not have been in this

place at all were it not for the futile, stagnant war and the glacial pace of the peace negotiations. We were living in an armed, amoral spiritual ghetto. Every investigation was its own little morality play set in a world where up was down, right was wrong, and good was bad. The whole damned country was one big extenuating circumstance. Even the real thieves and junkies and assailants and murderers seemed justified in copping a plea: Vietnam.

Guilty or innocent, their big mistake had been allowing themselves to be maneuvered into the army in the first place. They should have been home. Hell, we all should have been home, rebuilding our pathetic civilian lives one messed-up little piece at a time.

The more investigations I pulled, the angrier I got—angry at the army (which routinely put foolish young men in positions where they would screw up) or angry at the foolish young men themselves (who had so unquestioningly answered the army's clarion call to screw up). The symbiosis between the two was stupefyingly obvious. It had been part of the U.S. Army before Valley Forge. It will be part of the U.S. Army as long as there is a United States.

Additional duties came. Additional duties went. There was a suicide to investigate. A man died in a shootout with the military police on the steps of a cathouse just off post. There were drunks wandering around company compounds with loaded assault rifles. There were bar fights and heroin addicts on the nod. There were army doctors to interview—doctors who, asked for a cause of death, just shrugged their shoulders and said, "Search me, lieutenant. Bad luck. He just died." A distracted GI ran over a Vietnamese vehicle and killed twelve people. I filed my report. If I remember correctly, the army settled the claims for $1,200 each.

Nor was there a space on the investigation form to report that the soldier under investigation had been the victim of plain old government-issued bad luck. We were sad sacks. All of us. Life's clouds had rolled in and crapped down on us mightily. Usually,

132   THE MAJOR

it was a case of being in the wrong place at the wrong time. The whole country was the wrong place. The war was the wrong time.

Not that the army cared. Nobody cared. Looking up the chain of command, I could not see any sense of duty to these hapless young men whatsoever. There were only the wide, comfortable bottoms of uncaring bureaucrats and politicians all the way up to Kissinger and Nixon.

"You fix!" I wanted to yell up to the men at the top. "Now!"

But no. I was an officer and a gentleman by act of Congress. I could think these thoughts all I wanted, but duty and tenacious professionalism would not allow me to act or react. Not so much as a shoulder slump or a roll of the eyes.

The major reviewed our investigations and endorsed them forward to the colonel, who endorsed them forward to brigade, never to be seen again. At least we never saw them again. Often, the people up the line ignored the reports altogether. They awarded an Army Commendation Medal to the man who was killed on the whorehouse steps—dedication and bravery in pursuit of venery, I guess.

Then one day, they called me over to headquarters. The colonel wanted to see me. I trudged the two hundred yards through the heavy sand and walked in. The sergeant major looked up and jerked a thumb over his shoulder. They were waiting for me. Better get in there.

There were the colonel, the major, the adjutant, and the warrant officer who ran the personnel section. The colonel was holding a set of orders promoting me to captain. They had captain's bars ready to pin on me and everything. All I had to do was agree to stay in Vietnam six more months.

For a moment, I almost accepted. I had nothing at home. No one was waiting. More than two years of active duty had left a crater where civilian life had been. This was relatively good, safe, rear-echelon duty, and six months down the road a captaincy would look good on a civilian résumé.

But I couldn't do it. Standing there in front of the colonel, the major, and the rest of them, holding the orders, I had to say no. It was a sham, a ploy. If they could get a junior officer—any junior officer—to "re-up present duty," it would make the battalion look better at brigade level, the brigade look better at U.S. Army Vietnam, and so on. I wasn't that good an officer, but I wasn't that gullible either.

In fact, now that I thought about it, the whole deal was kind of insulting. I looked down at the name tag on my jungle fatigues just to make sure it said Lieutenant Smith, not Lieutenant Stupid. I thanked them, then handed the orders back to the personnel officer. Five minutes later, I was back at work in the motor pool.

The major became a little less tenaciously professional after that. It was still twelve-on, twelve-off, seven days a week, and he still meted out additional duties. But something changed. Something slumped. Time was ticking, and eventually my tour of duty came to an end.

He came over to the motor pool to say good-bye late one afternoon. It was kind of a personal honor, and I appreciated it. The motor pool was just about to close for the night. The sergeant of the guard had just posted the first two-man watch to the bunker and was beach-walking back to headquarters through the sand. One of the mechanics was inflating another South Vietnamese Army tire while a young Vietnamese soldier squatted, smoked, and looked on.

"What's it really about, Smitty?" the major asked. He leaned on his jeep. "I mean, here we are, busting our asses, and for what? Will it make any difference when we're gone?"

He trailed off, and we stood there for a few minutes watching the sun slide behind the artillery-scarred mountains across the bay on the mainland. Then he seemed to come to. He became the little bandy rooster again, shook my hand, and climbing behind the wheel of his jeep, he started the engine, put it in gear, and snapped off one last smart salute.

134   THE MAJOR

"Good luck, lieutenant," he said. "Proud to have served with you."

The last I saw of him, he had the jeep in four-wheel drive. The wheels ground through the deep sand by the gate, then caught the lip of the tar road, and he was gone.

"Fuck you," called a lizard in the scrub behind me. "Fuck you. Fuck you."

The Amnesty Barrel

We were going home. The high-mileage, retrofitted Boeing 707 sat out there on the tarmac, shimmering in the heat, the girl of our dreams, too good to be true—those low-slung swept wings, that classic silhouette. No airplane in history ever looked anywhere near as beautiful. We were standing in the air-conditioned sheet-metal shed that served as a boarding gate, looking out through the Plexiglas windows, ogling her. For our entire tour, she had been as unattainable as the homecoming queen. We had been homely hoodlums, the worthless dregs of the class. Now here she was, suddenly available, smiling coyly, saying, "What do you say, boys? Want to take me for a ride?"

The air force men in charge of the boarding process stood behind a plywood counter shuffling paper, killing time.

"All right. Listen up," one of them finally called in that tedious tone anyone who's ever been in the military associates with the first sergeant making announcements at morning formation. He pointed to a long red sign above the counter.

"This is a list of all the things you cannot—repeat—cannot—bring back into the United States of America."

We looked up at the sign, "Drugs," it said. "Weapons. Munitions. Plant materials. War souvenirs, including human body parts. Syringes." The sign went on at some length and in great detail.

"You will be searched upon arrival in the United States of America," the air force sergeant continued. "If you are found to

136

have any of these items on your person at the other end of this flight, you will be held as a member of the Armed Forces of the United States of America, charged, and prosecuted." He intoned the speech from sing-song rote memory. "Your separation from the armed forces will be delayed. You will serve time in a military prison after which you will be less than honorably discharged.

"If you have any of these items on your person now, you may drop them—no questions asked—over there in the amnesty barrel."

He and the rest of the air force staff pointed ensemble—like stewardesses directing our attention to the exits—to a red fifty-five-gallon drum near the door that opened onto the tarmac—the door to the airplane—the door home.

"No penalty. No charges. No questions asked. We're going to start boarding in ten minutes," he said. "You have ten minutes to think about it."

I've been thinking about the amnesty barrel off and on ever since. I've written it into short stories and essays. I've scratched it out of pieces and written it back in. I've used it as a symbol. I've given it up. I've returned to it. I've overworked the damn amnesty barrel like a second-rate picture in a Wednesday night continuing education watercolor class until everything runs together and everything is ruined yet again. It's an unusable, irresistible, heavy-handed, fifty-five-gallon allegory. God help me, I just can't leave it alone.

Look at it, standing there like a garbage can at the corner of Distrust and Disrespect. We'd been moral enough to ship off to war. Now the government was shaking us down, frisking us, threatening us, making sure we were moral enough to come home. You resented being treated like that, but then again, nobody left Vietnam with his naïveté intact. There were junkies, crooks, and thugs among us—maybe even murderers. We were heroes unless we were criminals. It was all so conflicted and confusing.

With less than five minutes to serve in the Republic of South

THE AMNESTY BARREL   137

Vietnam, I sidled over and glanced down into the amnesty barrel. There was heroin in there. A lot of it. Pure, strong heroin in those tiny two-dollar vials that would have been worth ninety dollars or more on the street in the States. The barrel was filled to a depth of six inches or more with those vials. And there were two pistols, Colt .45 automatics, and grenades and grenade-launcher rounds and knives and bayonets. There was one of those Fuji hats peasants wore out in the rice paddies. There weren't any body part souvenirs nesting atop the heroin. It was like an arcade claw-grab machine loaded with trouble.

I stole a glimpse around the room. A few men seemed to be struggling with something—maybe their consciences, maybe a more immediate sense of self-preservation. I moved away from the amnesty barrel to give them room to move in, and one or two of them did. As discreetly as possible they came up and tossed something into the barrel—as if they were making a wish at a shopping mall wishing well. Who knows? Maybe that's what the amnesty barrel was to them—a wishing well.

See how quickly the amnesty barrel starts to go rogue? The image is diabolical—all but impossible not to go overboard with it. It wasn't a wishing well. It was just a damn fifty-five-gallon drum painted red and perfectly positioned at a turning point in your life.

You were going home. You were at the gate—you and everything you had done to your soul. There was the amnesty barrel, there was the gate, and right out there, that beautiful plane and a free ride home to Mom and civilian life where no one knew anything about all this, where no one would ever know. You could drop anything you wanted into the barrel. They'd give you amnesty for it, no questions asked.

If only you could give yourself amnesty for everything you'd let them do to you—for not telling them to go to hell in the first place, for letting them steal two-plus years of your life, for coming to the realization that the government can and will screw with you as much as it wants whenever it wants and that you will submit to it, for conceding the point meekly, conceding it forever. For letting them beat you down, for letting them help you up, dust you off, and say, "Sorry 'bout that. Had to do it. Just part of the training. You OK?"

If only you could walk up and drop your self-knowledge into the amnesty barrel. You'd thought there were some things—morals, beliefs, and values—you would never compromise. You knew better now. You knew there was no amnesty barrel for what was wrong with you. You would have to smuggle your broken sense of self back into the States, where everyone who hadn't gone still held themselves in high esteem and was waiting.

The bored-sounding air force man called the flight. We lined up and walked past the amnesty barrel, out the door, across the sweltering tarmac, up the stairs, and onto the superheated plane. We jostled. We stowed gear. We crawled into the narrow little seats—as many seats as they could possibly fit on board. The plane smelled of sweat, cigarettes, airline meals, methane, and half-full toilets. It smelled of trip after trip, back and forth, day after day, year after year.

They closed the door, fired up the engines, and turned on the air. The temperature came down as we taxied out to the end of the runway, turned, and as full as we were, used every last foot to lift off. We cheered as the wheels broke free of the ground, and we looked out the windows at the Republic of South Vietnam disappearing behind us and the blue-gray of the sky merging with the blue-gray of the South China Sea, obscuring the horizon forever.

1972

It was a commune of psychologists—young PhD types—in South Minneapolis, and for a while after the war it was home. I'd found it through my job as a benefits counselor on the drug and alcohol ward at the Veterans Administration hospital. One of the psychologists worked there, and the rest—three or four others, the number rose and fell—used a combination of ever-so-slightly post-hippie idealism and gooey graduate school psychology to cohere to the commune.

We lived in a five-bedroom house across a quiet street from a dingy little Lithuanian Lutheran church. Between work and graduate school and social lives and romances, commune members were forever coming and going, but we tried to sit down and eat dinner together every evening.

There was also a once-a-week house meeting, where any issues were to be brought up and resolved—cooking and cleanup schedules, budgets, stereo volumes, noisy overnight guests—that sort of thing. There were those issues, and then there were the issues underlying those issues. If you were late with your share of the rent, someone in the group was apt to psychoanalyze you. Why were you displaying passive-aggressive tendencies? One PhD had a relationship with a slightly older woman. She was almost always there for dinner and almost always there for breakfast—and almost certainly a sign of something deeply oedipal.

One night at a house meeting, one of the PhD women relaxed

140

on the living room couch for five minutes pretending not to notice that one of her breasts had fallen completely out of her house-coat. She knew, all right. She had issues of her own. Finally, one of the PhD men pointed at her breast and asked in a simpy, snide, psychologist's voice, "Will you please put that thing away?"

The commune was my left-handed effort to reconnect with people who hadn't spent the past five years on the way into and out of Vietnam. Such a sad little dalliance. All it had cost was everything. No one else in my college crowd had gone. Their lives had proceeded unscathed, and I'd come home to find they'd cou-pled up, married, and settled down. The first babies had arrived while I was gone. One or two couples had bought houses. On the wall in the hallway outside the bathroom in a duplex one of the couples was renting, there was a homemade, felt-on-felt banner left over from their wedding—a wedding that had taken place while I was gone. It read, "We've only just begun."

My old college crowd was moving effortlessly into middle-class routines. There they were, building happy, productive lives, fully five years ahead of me.

"Think happy today," went the jingle for one of the local sav-ings and loans, and they were. My friends were all thinking happy today. They had only just begun to consume, to plan and save, to climb that career ladder, to move out of the city into the suburbs and small towns of middle America. In the two and a half years I had been gone, they had become latter-day lotus-eaters. I had become a second-rate Odysseus, bumbling and fumbling my way home to a place where no one was waiting.

Normal was surreal. Surreal was normal, palpably so. Here was my life—a crater. Nobody knew the trouble I'd seen, nor was anyone especially interested in hearing about it. They had no idea, none whatsoever. They listened when I tried to tell them. They paused for a moment, then went back to passing around baby pictures.

So I moved into the commune of psychologists thinking maybe

they could help me work through some of the crap so I, too, could start thinking happy today. My life was a clothesline sagging under a lot of wet, not especially clean laundry. Maybe I could use my brothers and sisters in the commune like those poles my grandmother used to prop up her clothesline on wash day.

The flawed assumption, of course, was that the psychologists would be sane and capable of thinking happy themselves, but they, too, were sagging clotheslines. The issues under their issues were real and layered, and now that they had lived communally for a while, their issues overlapped and entangled. If I expected any help with my problems from that direction, I would have to take a number.

Life sagged. Life sogged. Life lacked purpose and passion and direction. My job with the Veterans Administration reflected this perfectly. I helped recovering alcoholics and junkies register for education benefits and other programs. I was the interlocutor between the VA and the chaos of life on the ward, in the halfway house, or back on the street.

The futility ... Time and again, we would get an addict detoxified, set his feet on the path to recovery, put a chemical-free spring in his step, a shine on his shoes, and a melody back in his heart only to have him slide back into his old ways.

One baby-faced junkie, a heroin addict from my old unit in Vietnam, went through the inpatient program, got assigned to a halfway house, and began going to school only to succumb to the call of the streets. Strung out again, he held up a gas station, and as he ran toward his car afterward, he shoved a sawed-off shotgun down his trouser leg and shot himself in the knee. The last time I saw him, he was handcuffed to his hospital bed at County General, a guard at his door. He was indignant that the doctor wouldn't increase his medication to a level he personally felt would be sufficient to numb the pain. He was also indignant that the gas station attendant he'd threatened to murder had found the situation so funny.

142   1972

He too had only just begun—he and legions of others: mendacious methadone patients, relapsed twelve-steppers, alcoholics, constipated opiate abusers, jittery speed freaks, lovers of barbiturates, scammers of systems, con artists.

The chemical dependency program and the inner city were full of needle-marked needy people shooting drugs, shooting angles, and shooting each other. They were the war in Vietnam as I had known it—stupid and senseless, a crater and a complete waste of time.

I might have come home, found a job with a future and a nice girl. I might have married and tried to think happy today—or at the very least, once married, tried to restrict the unhappy thinking to the small hours of the morning. But I didn't belong. I knew who I really was. I knew what I really was. I knew my breaking points, and I knew with absolute certainty that the government could make me do anything it wanted me to do whenever it wanted me to do it. I had no illusions—or at the very least I had a different set of illusions than the lotus-eaters. I could not subsist on lotuses, accept good fortune, or live what passed for a normal life. I couldn't only just begin.

One of the women in the commune had a hope chest. She'd filled it with sheets and blankets and housewares—stuff she planned to bring to the normal life she would lead when she found the right man, married, and settled down.

Hope. The idea was as cloying as your grandmother's lavender perfume and served the same purpose. The world was awash in the smell of sad and saggy old meat. Any hope you might stumble across masked the smell and kept reality at bay for a little while.

Somewhere in this period, somehow, writing became a refuge. I fell heir to an old manual typewriter and discovered they sold typing paper at Red Owl—greasy-feeling "erasable" typing paper. After supper on nights when there were no house meetings or other issues for the commune to resolve, I would go to my room, close the door, chain-smoke, and mill sheet after sheet of the stuff through the machine.

I can't remember what I wrote about. Nothing remains, not one jot, and I for one am damned happy it doesn't. For quite a while, I tended to drink cheap Scotch and write. The gift of tongues descended on me. Damn, I was one clever bastard on Scotch. Only the following morning would I discover those deep thoughts and bon mots had been neither deep nor especially *bon*.

Still, draft after draft, the drek piled up. I could go back through the drafts and watch simple sentences evolve into more complex thoughts and paragraphs. I could observe how words and phrases went together—or failed to go together. I was teaching myself to play the typewriter by ear.

Elsewhere in the house, in their rooms in their beds in the dark, listening to the clatter and clack of my typewriter, the hippie psychologists wrestled with their own hopes and demons. Outside, in the city night, in bars, on street corners, and in cheap apartment house hallways, the junkies stuck in needles and fixed and planned their next fuckups: Who to scam? What drugstore or gas station to stick up? Out in the suburbs, the lotus-eaters nodded off to sleep with questions of their own: What color do we paint the kitchen? Now that the baby is here, how much more life insurance do we take out on Bob? Should we buy the all-new AMC Matador or the Chevy Vega wagon?

For some reason—I was probably working out a twist in the ham-handed plot of some unsalable short story—I decided to take a walk one evening. I remember it was a fellowship night at the Lithuanian Lutheran Church—a lot of large, not-quite-assimilated-looking Lithuanian men and long-suffering women were mingling on the lawn before going into the church itself.

My walk took me south, through the heart of blue-collar single-family-residence Minneapolis. I trudged past block after block of well-maintained little houses—houses built to accommodate immigrant Swedes, Norwegians, and others who'd come to

Minnesota in the early twentieth century, found work, and established a toehold in America. This was dull, taupey, stucco South Minneapolis. Bikes-on-the-front-lawn Minneapolis, flawed only by the airport runway noise three miles to the southeast and the steady stream of planes overhead. The Minneapolis that had fed South and Roosevelt high schools its best and its brightest. The Minneapolis that had sent so many sons off to fight World War II—sons who came home, found girls, married, and struck out for the sprawling Levittown-inspired plains of Richfield, where they bought houses and raised families of their own.

I remember thinking I could have been born and raised there. I might have fit in there had the cards been shuffled and dealt ever so slightly differently. I remember walking all the way to Minnehaha Creek and turning left, continuing along the parkway between Lake Nokomis and Hiawatha Golf Course, and turning north, back toward the commune.

I remember seeing the little one-bedroom house on the narrow lot overlooking Lake Hiawatha and Hiawatha Park on Twenty-Eighth Avenue South and the For Sale sign. They wanted fifteen thousand dollars for it. I offered eleven. We settled at thirteen-five. Two weeks later, the typewriter and I moved in.

A Typewriter Reverie

I am writing this in Microsoft Word—the Coupe de Ville of word processing programs. I'm cruising on automatic. If this sentence takes a wide turn or heads up a dead end, I'll highlight it, hit "delete," and I'll be back at the beginning, just to the right of the period from the last sentence, the cursor patiently blinking at me, asking, "Where to?"

If I misspell a word, the program underlines it in red. It underlines sentence fragments, too. It questions some commas and, occasionally, homonyms. The use of the passive voice is routinely discouraged, as are a whole raft of other unstylish elements of style.

Microsoft Word. The tenth-grade English teacher I never had.

Sometimes, a window pops open, and a little animated computer starts gently correcting me via cartoon balloons. The computer icon is a cheerful but pedantic little bastard. I click it shut as fast as it shows up. I've searched the pull-down menus high and low for a box I can check that will turn it off for good, but Microsoft has it grubbed down in there pretty darned good. Too damned good for an old fart like me.

Or should that be "well"? The little computer will no doubt show up and try to tell me when I spell-check this later.

I am one of a dwindling number of people who learned to write on manual typewriters. Not some god-awful IBM electric model but a real manual typewriter where you pounded the keys hard and rammed the carriage back to the right and ratcheted the

146

page up at the end of each line, going through ream after ream of yellow second-sheet paper in the process.

A manual typewriter was a writer's typewriter. You could sit there and feed your addictions to coffee, cigarettes, and American English all at the same time. You took a slug of coffee and a drag off your Camel. You stared moodily at the notch where the keys rose to strike the page, and you waited. Another slug. Another drag. You wrote a halting half sentence. And so it would go—hour after hour, pot after pot, Camel after Camel.

Your addiction to alcohol would have to wait until you were done writing for the day. Drinking and writing on a manual typewriter didn't mix. The alcohol made you think you were classing your stuff up. You pulled the page from the machine and smirked. Damn, you were clever. But you hated yourself the next morning when you read what you'd written.

There was a scratch and heft to writing on a manual typewriter. It was a deliberate process, and it gave your words weight—weight they don't have when you see them on the computer screen. And you couldn't just lightly touch the keys the way you did on an electric typewriter. You had to hammer them hard. And once you'd tattooed a word onto the page, it was there to stay, unless you went back and x-ed it out.

My father, the newspaper rewrite man, typed with the index and second fingers of both hands. When he x-ed out something in his copy, he would overstrike it with x's and o's.

xoxoxoxoxoxoxoxo

The left index finger was for x. The right was for o. Working in tandem, they were much quicker than just going *xxxx*, and quicker was important when you were on deadline for the next edition.

I came to love manual typewriters and writing when I visited the newsroom as a child. My brothers and I would take the train downtown to go to a baseball game after my father finished work. We would usually arrive in the newsroom as the last edition of the day went to bed. Something about the work and the men who did it felt heroic. The scene was a living WPA bas-relief mural. The men on the city desk had shirt sleeves rolled up well past their elbows, collars unbuttoned, and neckties jerked loose off to one side. Wire service teletypes banged; bells rang. The manual typewriters were as big and old and dirty as the city itself, the keys as mysterious as the stops on a church organ. Equally grubby old-fashioned headsets hung close by, connected to dial telephones, ready for a rewrite man to slap them on, spin a book of carbon paper and yellow copy paper into the typewriter carriage, and take a story from a reporter in the field.

"Get me a quote, Rooney. Put the damn phone down, go back in there, and get me a quote."

Ashtrays overflowed with smoldering cigarette butts. Wastebaskets overflowed and smoldered too. There were half-empty cups of cold vending machine coffee at every elbow, ready to be spilled at precisely the wrong moment, and long library sheers and pots of rubber cement—not the cut-and-paste icons on the word processing menu bar, but real scissors and real rubber cement—ready to cut and paste the updated lead on the story at the top of page one of the next edition.

This was how real writing felt. You pounded it out. It was manual labor you did with your brain. This was how real writing smelled—like the city, like truck exhaust and the press room downstairs and cigarette smoke and BO and the three drinks the copy editor bolted down with his corned beef on rye around the corner an hour ago, all of it blended together and wafting around on the meager breeze from the oscillating fan on the column above the city desk.

This was what I wanted to do when I grew up. I wanted to write: to play the manual typewriter as if it were a piano, to make words flow out and float across the room the way musical notes scrolled and floated up and away from musicians in the comics. If I couldn't write for a newspaper, then I would write somewhere else. I would play the typewriter. That's all I ever wanted to do.

On nights when my father brought work home, he would take the Remington portable down from the front closet shelf and set up shop on the coffee table in the living room. We would fall asleep to his four-fingered clack-and-pause rhythm. To us, it was as peaceful and sweet and right as summer rain on the roof.

Every so often, you see a microchip word slinger—someone who cut their teeth on a word processor—pause and look at an old manual typewriter in a museum or on a shelf somewhere. They press a key or two out of curiosity—push it halfway down and watch with detached curiosity as a letter rises halfway to the notch. Or maybe they punch a word or two onto the page very tentatively.

They seem to be afraid they'll break the machine. They don't know that the manual typewriter, as perfected sometime in the first quarter of the twentieth century, is one of the most durable pieces of communications machinery the human race has ever mass-produced. Generations of writers—good, bad, and indifferent—have beaten the crap out of manual typewriters even as they have poured their hearts into them. They've picked them up, dropped them, and thrown them out the residential hotel window, over the fire escape railing, down three floors into the street. They treated them the way Jerry Lee Lewis treated pianos. Those typewriters endured. The manual typewriter may well represent the high-water mark of the Industrial Revolution.

Which is not to say there were not lemons. The portable Olivetti I took to college was a terrible machine—underengineered and flimsy from the very beginning. It lost keys for no reason. They just fell out. By the time the Olivetti and I graduated, we were down to the alphabet and basic punctuation marks, except for the colon and semicolon key. Necessity became the mother of invention again, and I learned to hyphenate my way around the problem.

The more you wrote on manual typewriters, the more you came to prefer one brand over another. I was a Royal typewriter man. Down deep, I suppose I still am. A Royal was a four-square machine—solid and formidable, a rock with a keyboard. Everything you needed was where you could get at it, including a lever that reversed the direction the ribbon was traveling and another that adjusted the height of the ribbon as it passed behind the notch where the keys struck. The idea was to even out wear on the ribbon and extend its life. The younger and poorer you were, the more mileage you tried to coax out of a ribbon.

The only design flaw I ever found on a Royal manual typewriter was a feature called the Magic Margin—a tab up near the knob you twisted to turn the platen. If you touched the Magic Margin tab at the wrong time, a spring-loaded device that set the margin width would slam shut, leaving only an inch-wide column down the middle of the page where you could type. There was some simple but hidden way to readjust the width, but you had to stop and figure it out. Since you only made the mistake two or three times a year, you forgot how to correct it. So you sat there and swore at the machine and fidgeted with all the levers and buttons until you remembered. Meanwhile, on the page, the brilliant thought or sentence you'd been working on when you accidentally hit the Magic Margin would be sitting there, cooling off.

In spite of the Magic Margin, the Royal manual was the machine of choice for my flawed and suffering young genius and me. I bought my first at a garage sale. It cost four dollars and seventy-five cents. It had the temperament of a punch-drunk boxer hanging around the gym looking for work as a sparring partner. That Royal and I went hundreds of rounds while I trained. For a long time, we worked all night every night, chewing through ream after ream of that yellow paper, false-starting short stories, flexing metaphors until they broke, writing long, florid sentences, then backspacing and x-o-ing them into simple subject-verb-object things.

When you learn to write on a manual typewriter, you begin to listen for the manual typewriter in other writers' stuff. Nelson Algren wrote, "Never play cards with a man called Doc. Never eat at a place called Mom's. Never sleep with a woman whose troubles are worse than your own." A manual-typewriter writer can hear Algren's machine in the tempo. A sentence. A pause. Another sentence. A longer pause. Then the bangety-bang. You can almost hear the keys clatter. You can almost hear him slam the carriage back to the right with a flourish at the end. Let's see you do that in Microsoft Word.

The rhythm is in the mechanism. Hit and hold the shift key, and the carriage rises a quarter inch. Let the shift key go, and the carriage drops. Do it once, and it will give you an iamb—a single, two-syllable foot of poetry. Do it five times in a row, and you've got a line of iambic pentameter.

Shakespeare says, "That time of year thou may in me behold..."

The typewriter goes, "Clunk-clunk, clunk-clunk, clunk-clunk, clunk-clunk, clunk-clunk..."

You make words a keystroke at a time, stringing them along the line until, a few spaces before the end of the line, a bell rings, "bing." You slam the carriage back to the right and begin clunk-clunking and keystroking your way along the next line. Words become sentences. Sentences become paragraphs. Paragraphs become pages. There's a gratification to it—a sense of fulfillment. Now you're getting somewhere.

Writing on a computer feels slippery and plastic by comparison. A typewriter churns out pages of real paper—hard copy. You can go back through your drafts, compare and refine phrases. On a computer, you revise everything on the same draft. You lose good stuff to your own revisions.

On the bright side, the computer will make sure everything is spelled fairly well. It may let a few homonyms slip through now and then, but if you're diligent as you spell-check, you can be reasonably sure the grammar will be all right and that everything will be punctuated pretty competently.

Something about spell-check seems to make people want to use big words badly, to just throw them in, make sure they're spelled correctly, and hope they're appropriate. Call it erudition through obfuscation. "He must be smart. Look at all the big words he's using."

Something about writing on a manual typewriter made you gravitate toward small words, simple sentences, and short paragraphs. They sounded smarter, got the point across more clearly, and got the job done with a little more flair. It was the "dare to be clear" school of writing—a high-wire act where readers understood you the first time through your copy, an act of deliberate intellectual nonconformity, a way to goose the system.

It's gone now. Gone forever. My cursor blinks. It marks time. I will only get so far into this century. Then my cursor will freeze. My screen will fade for good. When that time comes, I will return to the twentieth century and spend eternity there, one more in an infinite number of simians hunkered in front of an infinite number of Royal manual typewriters, staring at the notches, waiting for those muses to drop by and crap pearls.

Advertising Memories

"I really like where your head is at," the first advertising creative director to hire me said as he offered me a job. He was a hoary old advertising copywriter, and he had no qualms about using clichés or hanging prepositions off the end of his sentences as long as it sold. He had the bright red complexion of a practicing alcoholic. We were in his office, in that low point between his three-martini lunch and cocktail hour. I had been suffering for my art as a real writer, and I had holes in both shoes as well as in both my cheap black cotton socks. I kept both feet flat on the floor.

He had seen something in the writing samples and speculative ad campaigns I had shown him. I did not know what it was at the time. I do now. He had seen the ten miles of broken glass across which I had to crawl in order to establish contact with the rest of the human race. He had seen my junk drawer of a mind. He had seen the way I could rummage around in there and come up with some "growing up in the Midwest" experience or some analogy glimpsed through a mirror darkly—an experience or analogy that might help one of the agency's clients to appear more clever and sell more stuff. He had seen the narrow, frayed, rope bridge of humor and light-hearted whimsy that was my writing style and how that style spanned the gorge between others and me. He had seen the river of alcohol flowing in the mists far below, and he had known he would be able to deal with me, alcoholic to alcoholic.

153

Advertising had been good to him. He was rich enough to keep horses and bed the kind of middle-aged ingénues who love horses. He had become a fine judge of horseflesh because he had become a fine judge of advertising writers and art directors, and here I was, a promising young emotional gelding, an intriguing addition to his creative stable. He really liked where my head was at.

I took the job, and minutes after I started, I knew that—in the creative department at least—I was among fellow travelers. There were brooding, paranoid workaholics. There were brooding, paranoid alcoholics. There were highly competitive schemers and overeducated, chip-on-the-shoulder, unpublished but professorial poets and failed novelists. There was a stunningly beautiful ice queen of an art director. There was an over-the-hill, raspy-voiced, chain-smoking woman writer with a fainting couch in her office and a come-hither presence that scared the crap out of me. There were a couple of big-eyed, small-voiced vamps— cast-off Daddy's girls with loose morals and self-esteem issues. There were dope-smoking, acetone-buzzed art directors and key-liners finessing type to Pink Floyd cassettes for hours at a time.

Every damned one of us was brilliantly flawed in some unique way. We were inadequate or abnormal or socially autistic or too bright for our own goddamned good. We were—each of us—willing to walk through fire to prove ourselves worthy of something— anything—in the eyes of the creative director, agency management, and the rest of the human race.

We had cracks and fissures. Genius seeped, sometimes bubbled, and on rare occasions flowed through those fissures. The creative director—indeed, the entire advertising agency—prospered because of our seeping genius. It was a satanic symbiosis.

The creative director and his account service director partner—the two men who owned the place—fostered an ingenious culture and nurtured our anxieties. They tended individual flaws in the way that best suited you as an individual. They did whatever it took to maximize your genius flow. If you needed to be admired and told you were a genius, they admired you and told you that you were a genius. If you needed to be reminded you were a worthless piece of shit, they reminded you that you were a worthless piece of shit. If you needed a company car, they got you a company car. If you needed to feel unworthy of a company car, they somehow managed to do that, too. Had you needed a daily high colonic from a bare-breasted nurse, I am sure they would have gotten you a daily high colonic from a bare-breasted nurse. I was working in a Weimar-era cabaret whorehouse where flawed and failed people lived the fantasies and fetishes they needed to live in order to keep that high-grade advertising bullshit flowing out through their fissures.

Me? I needed to be on the outside, to be excluded from any discussion of direction for the creative department or the agency at large, to be a copywriting Achilles and brood in my tent down the shore, away from the larger army of which I was part. So they fashioned a cauldron of angst especially for me. They gave me my own, perpetual, self-renewing case of the office politics willies. They had meetings behind closed doors without inviting me. They hired and fired people without asking me.

In exchange, I showed *them*. Boy howdy. I busted my ass twelve billable hours a day. I came in on weekends and worked like a dog.

The two owners were macho. So were the phalanx of men immediately below them on the organization chart and the phalanx of men below that. It was one big daisy chain of a guy's club, where everyone drank hard and wrestled with one another at company parties and hunted and fished together. The place was awash in Eddie Bauer upper-middle-class white-guy faux testosterone.

As manly as those guys thought they were, only one of them had been in the military, and none of them had been to Vietnam. At lunch or over drinks after work, they used to brag about how they had evaded the draft. Nothing made you feel like you fit in quite like sitting around with a bunch of comfortable young rich guys while they bragged about dodging the war that had cost you everything.

The owners were lechers. They roamed the halls copping what they considered to be playful feels from the young women who worked for them. I stood by and watched them do it. I stood by when I should have said or done something because I was a coward.

I loathed myself, but I loathed the guy's club more. I at least knew it was wrong to cop feels from your employees. But God seemed to have shipped the guy's club guys without installing moral gyroscopes. They didn't care that the owners were copping feels. They even copped feels themselves when they thought they could get away with it. I could not allow myself to be one of them; still, I craved some sort of respect from them. This was the fissure through which my good advertising stuff flowed—and it turned out it was really good stuff. I was a natural. I was throwing high-inside fastballs—the hot stinking cheddar—and in no time at all, I was winning advertising awards. Headhunters and other creative directors began to call. They, too, liked where my head was at.

"You're going to be something," the middle-aged, raspy-voiced, chain-smoking advertising copywriting seductress told me. She patted a place beside her on the fainting couch. Afraid she would try to cop a feel, I declined. I can still hear the long strands of love beads that hung in her doorway clicking and clinking behind me as I escaped.

I struck up a friendship with a fellow inmate in the asylum—a slightly older, infinitely more acerbic guy. He became my Virgil, and he showed me around this hell one ring at a time.

"How come there are no old copywriters?" I asked him one afternoon. His office was across the hall from mine. We were standing in our respective doorways, killing time, smoking, letting the creative juices simmer.

"Aw, don't worry about that," he told me. "You won't have that problem. You can actually write. You will be on your deathbed and some account man will show up with just one more copy change he needs to make for the client. There'll be a couple of nurses in the corner. One will turn to the other and whisper in hushed tones, 'The old fart is incontinent, but he can still write.'"

Virgil and I were in awe of the ice queen art director. She was extremely talented, beautiful, remote, and intimidating. There was an aura of pedantry and virtue about her. Working on an ad with her was like collaborating with your kindergarten teacher. She was daunting. You were on your best behavior and watched your language. When she went out of town for photo shoots or to produce television commercials, we would sneak into her office, fart, and say words like "fuck."

The place was an incubator. A Petri dish sprouting a fecund culture rooted in equal parts anxiety, hormones, and perpetual adolescence. Grown men walked the halls, knuckles raw from hitting the rough-hewn plank walls. There were intricate, strained, obvious office affairs in which people cheated on people with whom they had cheated on their spouses while the owners enforced an abstract moral code arbitrarily. You could bang any and everyone, provided your fissures were oozing and you were of value to the company. If you were not of value or not in great favor, they would take false offense and use your affair as an excuse to fire you.

It felt like the other shoe was always about to drop. The whole place was skating on thin ice atop a vast lake of bad karma, and when I couldn't take it any more, I took a job with another agency.

Two months later, the first agency burned to the ground. It wasn't Sodom and Gomorrah—God didn't smite the place; it was probably arson. The building had been a small brownstone, and the agency had a long-term lease. Two years after the fire, a skyscraper stood on the site.

The new agency liked where my head was at. I had thought—naively it turned out—that the new agency would be better, more stable, and more moral and virtuous. I had hoped it would make me better, more stable, and more moral and virtuous as well. Nope. Two years later, I moved on to another agency. Eighty-nine days later, a fourth agency, and eighteen months after that, it was back to the first agency—at a new location and under new ownership and management. The new guys running the place were surrounded by the usual double phalanx of guy's clubbers. I resumed my role as Achilles—more senior this time, but still alone and still sulking. They had it all set up so my fissures could flow.

When I left that agency for the second time, I went into business for myself, which is where I am now. I am my own owner and creative director, and some days I really like where my head is at. Some days I don't. At least the owner doesn't cop feels in front of me. He sits—more patiently these days—beside the old fissures, and he catches the seepage in an old bucket, and he carries it off to his quiet little handful of clients.

When Achilles shows up for work all sulky, I tell him to take the day off.

Almost

I don't do well in groups—never have, never will. Set me down in the middle of a room full of people, and I will immediately begin to edge toward the door. I will edge as inconspicuously as possible, but take my word for it, I will edge. I have no need to offend anyone. There is only that overwhelming need to slip out, jerk my necktie loose, unbutton my collar, and run.

All those people interacting, talking, mingling, drive me ever deeper into myself, where I become my own voyeur, at once fascinated and horrified by my dilemma and my many social ineptitudes.

Some people thrive in crowds. They move through the room effortlessly, pausing to talk with an individual here, melding into a small group there, listening, laughing, shaking a hand, slapping a back, fitting in flawlessly. My wife is like that. She has her own warm, confident gravitational pull. People are drawn to her. She radiates. Meanwhile, if you look across the room, you will see me edge ever closer to the door.

I have edged toward the door at high school dances and college mixers. I have edged toward the door at religious services and precinct caucuses, at weddings and funerals. Long ago, when I was single, I edged toward the door on dates. I've edged toward conference room doors in business meetings in swanky Manhattan skyscrapers. Naked as the day the Great Spirit created me,

I've edged toward the door—a blanket flap actually—in a Native American sweat lodge in Montana. When I run into neighbors at the local post office, even as I say hello, I start saying good-bye and edging toward the door. I just don't do well in groups, no matter how good or pleasant or holy or noble the cause. I would start a group devoted to distrusting the dynamics of groups, but we can all see where that would lead, can't we?

Consider the evening I spent alone and in anguish in the middle of a big group in a ballroom at the Waldorf Astoria—a group of advertising people from prestigious advertising agencies all over the country. The Magazine Publishers Association of America was honoring the twenty-five most creative magazine advertising campaigns of the year. They were going to award $100,000 to the writer and art director who'd created the best campaign.

It was shameless on the Magazine Publishers' part. A gimmick, a perverse, masturbatory, reflexive verb of a promotion intended to get the entire American advertising community to think about magazine advertising. I didn't want to attend—not even when one of the campaigns I'd written had been named to the top twenty-five. Three weeks and two thousand miles from the Waldorf, I had already started to edge toward the door.

But then a young woman from the Magazine Publishers called and urged my art director partner and me to attend. She said she thought we really ought to be there. In the social conventions that attend advertising award shows, a call from the committee suggesting you should attend is often a coded message to the winner: "Be there to pick up the swag. Don't stiff us."

My art director partner and I were skeptical but vain enough to take the bait, go to the strip mall, rent tuxedos, head for New York, and check into the Waldorf.

Cocktails were at six, and as we registered for the fete, someone handed us our seating assignment. We were at table 1, seats 1 and 2. A good omen? Maybe, we thought, and we wandered off to find a cocktail hour bottle of beer. Before we could shoulder our way to the cash bar, however, someone from the Magazine Publishers swept us up and took us to meet a couple of the judges.

"I voted for your campaign," one of the judges gushed. "I thought it was the best thing I've ever seen."

My buddy and I toted up the omens. They called and urged us to be there. Table 1, seats 1 and 2. At least one judge voted for our campaign. So what if we were standing there in a couple of tuxes that had spent last Saturday night at the head table at a Holiday Inn wedding dinner in Fridley, Minnesota? The more the cocktail-hour-at-the-Waldorf beer flowed, the less cynical we became, and when we sat down at table 1 and found out the young woman in seat 3 was one of only five people in the room who knew which campaign had won the big prize, we were damned near ready to toss our last doubt overboard.

The dinner was interminable. The entertainment was interminable and insufferable. Buster Poindexter and his band performed a prolonged version of their one hit, "Hot-Hot-Hot." Someone had adapted the lyrics to talk about magazine advertising being hot, and just when we thought the band would wrap it up, they left the stage and congaed around the ballroom for ten minutes. The longer the number lasted, the more surreal it became. Faces in the crowd—faces of people who'd embraced cocktail hour a little too fervently and finished off the carafes of table wine at dinner—appeared manically, almost insanely amused, like the faces in some kaleidoscoping arts movie montage where the nightclubbing goes tragically, alcoholically awry.

Hot-hot-hot. Magazines were hot-hot-hot. It was all cleavage and hips and drums and mariachis and too-colorful, ruffled shirt sleeves and sensory overload. I found myself channeling Poindexter. I imagined him whining to his agent over the telephone saying, "Christ, Bernie. The Magazine Publishers? Hot-hot-hot? Why don't you just kill me?"

I was pushing my chair back to start edging toward the door when Buster Poindexter and his band finally returned to the stage and wrapped it up. The masters of ceremony stepped out of the wings and began the award presentation. I pulled my chair back in. Hot damn. Here we go.

Their presentation proved as interminable and insufferable as the band, with a twenty-minute pitch on magazine advertising, followed by ten minutes on how the competition was judged, followed by three minutes of gushing over each of the twenty-five finalist campaigns, including shining spotlights on the teams that created them. There I sat, at table 1, seat 1, listening not so much to the presentation as to that crowd-averse internal soliloquy of mine. I hurtled between vanity and skepticism. This could be it. No, it couldn't. We were hot-hot-hot. We were not-not-not. We were a couple of hacks from the Midwest. There was the stage. There was the door.

The big moment came, teetered on the brink for the length of a drum roll. And the winner was . . .

Not us.

The spotlight shined down on a hip young creative team at a table in the back of the room—too hip for strip mall tuxedoes— from Portland, Oregon. Theirs had been one of three campaigns for Nike in the show—campaigns that had cost more to photograph than ours had cost to run in those hot-hot-hot magazines. Even as they pushed past us at table 1, I was pushing away from the table, unclipping the strip mall tuxedo bow tie, unbuttoning the collar on the starch-fronted shirt, shaking hands with other people at the table, edging toward the door.

Northwest Airline's flights for Minneapolis left from gate 10 at LaGuardia in those days—at the end of a concourse, with a dirty-windowed view of the Midtown skyscrapers in the distance. It was usually a who's who of a gate, and whether you were coming or going, you almost always ran into other Twin Cities advertising people. Mercifully, no one else was at gate 10 waiting to go back to Minneapolis the next morning, and when the plane came in from Minneapolis, no one we knew got off. We took one last look at the city in the distance, and carrying our rumpled tuxedos in cheap strip mall tuxedo store garment bags, we boarded the plane.

"Told you so," skeptic me told vain me all the way home. The rest of me edged toward the door. I don't do well in groups.

Pimping My Muse

From time to time back before I became one of the new has-beens of advertising, I used to go talk to advertising school classes about creativity. There they would be, all those fresh-faced, eager young minds out to master the alchemy of advertising, pens poised, ready to take down every word and thought. There I would be, regretting my role in encouraging them.

"Go back," I wanted to stage-whisper to them. "It's a trick. If you have any talent at all, someday you'll regret wasting it in advertising."

But the young people with the poised pens weren't there to hear that. They wanted to learn how to be creative. They or their parents had paid thousands of dollars for them to go to ad school, and they expected more than a punch-drunk old ad man felt the subject deserved—more respect, more thought, more inspiration.

Here were advertising's true acolytes. They thought it was an art form and that advertising copywriters and art directors were creative gods who deserved to be treated as a breed apart; they fervently hoped that someday they, too, would be able to flaunt eccentricities and cash in on whatever talent they had in the hothouse culture of an ad agency creative department. What they wanted from me—what I had been brought in to deliver—was a set of moves that, once applied to their sample creative pieces, would land them their first job in advertising, as if that first job were a level to beat in a video game.

I couldn't bring myself to burst their bubble. I couldn't tell them that, in advertising, as in other so-called creative endeavors, persistence plus mediocrity trump true creativity every time. In advertising, as elsewhere in life, the truly creative person has neither the focus nor the tenacity to succeed.

Advertising creativity has always seemed pampered, pretentious, self-indulgent, and mediocre to me—the triumph of form over substance.

Well, that's not exactly true. It hasn't *always* seemed that way. For the first couple of weeks, it did seem pretty fun and important. The veneer was thin, though, and soon it began to crack and peel. This wasn't creative. Not really.

In real advertising, the truly creative person wanders the halls in a fog, an idiot savant, inept, isolated. Then one day, under the pressure of a deadline or with a big account on the line for the entire agency, lightning will strike or their muse will crap an advertising pearl, and the truly creative person will give birth to the idea that saves the day. Everyone will say "oooh" and "ahhh" for a moment, admiring the little skyrocket the genius touched off as it bursts overhead. Then some less talented, more persistent "creative" person will steal the bolt from the blue and take all the credit for it, leaving the truly creative person to disappear back into that fog and wander some more.

You know how some ants keep aphids for the honeydew they secrete? In advertising, real creative people are the aphids. The persistent but mediocre people are the ants.

"Nothing in the world can take the place of Persistence," that most mediocre of American presidents Calvin Coolidge said. "Talent will not; nothing is more common than unsuccessful men with talent. Genius will not; unrewarded genius is almost a proverb. Education will not; the world is full of educated derelicts. Persistence and determination alone are omnipotent. The slogan 'Press On' has solved and always will solve the problems of the human race."

I could have preached the gospel of persistence to those eager young minds, but as an unsuccessful man, an unrewarded genius, and an educated derelict, I didn't want to give Coolidge the satisfaction. It would have sounded bitter. Besides, the persistent but mediocre students in the class would have known this already, and the truly creative people would never figure it out. Their talent is the baby from whom the persistent but mediocre perpetually take candy.

Standing in front of the class, preaching the gospel of creativity, horror lay out there in front of me in layers, each layer exuding its own wince and tang. All those young people, relatively bright, and eager to sell their souls to corporate commerce. Oy.

What is advertising creativity if not striking a Faustian deal with the multinational corporations? What do advertising creative people do other than painting a human face on the conglomerates—turning them into sweet-faced plastic blow-up dolls for consumers to put their arms around as they sit on their couches and watch television?

"C'mon...What's the code?" the students always seemed to be asking. "How can we make people want what the corporations are selling? New cars, new insurance, new shoes, new bodies, underwear, teeth, a new brand of beer. How can we make people need these things and make them unhappy if they can't have them?"

They were young and unhorrified. They didn't care that genius once prostituted is prostituted forever—the tough stain will always be there on your soul. Nothing Procter & Gamble makes will get rid of it. You'll never be able to Shout it out.

No business on earth, including the entertainment industry, has as many award shows as advertising. Standing up there, proselytizing, I often found myself speaking in award tongues. "Blah-blah this show. Blah-blah that show." I presented awards and award shows as the goals—the bright, shiny objects they were pursuing. I held awards up like a stick. I waved them in the air and told those ad classes, "Here it is! Go fetch!"

I didn't tell them that one revered advertising friend of mine—a man who has won more advertising awards than some highly successful New York ad agencies have—has taken to calling the award shows "Clever Fest." I didn't tell them that winning a big award was like winning a prize from the second row at a baseball and milk jug throwing game on the carnival midway. Five minutes later, the glow is gone.

I was horrified, too, to think I might inadvertently encourage a real genius to bastardize real talent. Was I urging some future Van Gogh or Scott Fitzgerald to go into ads?

Then there was the horror of critiquing their student work—of looking at their portfolios and offering insights and advice. Most of the work was derivative. It was based on advertising campaigns they had seen in award shows, as well it should have been. They were students, after all, and they were just finding their own styles and voices. I would look at their layouts and storyboards and fight the urge to recoil. I wanted to run from the room and hide on the fire escape. But I owed them some form of positive feedback if at all possible.

"Nice thought," I would tell a young writer. "Try finding a stronger way to say it. Write it fifty different ways, then pick the version that just plain says it better."

"Is there a better visual metaphor to use here?" I would suggest to a young art director. "Something more cutting and elegant? Keep looking. Be persistent."

I was helping to create the next generation of clever people. Pimping my muse—and showing them how they, in turn, might pimp theirs. Did they sense my conflict? Could they feel me saying, "Go back. It's a trick"? Or "No! Wait! Here it is, kid! Secondrate fame and fortune! See it? C'mon boy! Here it is! Fetch!"

I always thought that, as inevitably happens to all advertising creative people, when I found myself crapped from the giant back end of the business, I would build one of those backyard grottoes complete with a bathtub shrine sheltering an award show statuette.

I have the time now. I'm one of the new has-beens. I even went so far as to start looking for my old awards. When I couldn't find them, I asked my wife. She told me to go look in those boxes out in the garage.

Karma Turd A-Coming

For a while there, I was a vice president associate creative director at a highly creative advertising agency—VP, ACD. I'd worked hard, and it seemed like a weighty title at first. I'll confess to a spate of even larger than normal narcissism. And for a while I had to push hard to get my ego through the door into any room.

But the people in charge hadn't given me any equity with the title. They held executive committee meetings without me, after which they walked around looking spookily owlish, tracking puddles of collusion through the halls. Clearly they had big, scary secrets they were not going to share with me. In short order, my ego deflated. My narcissism sagged. It quickly became clear I wasn't their kind of guy and this was the end of the line. They weren't going to vote me into their club. They voted instead to sell the agency to a British conglomerate, and after the sale, they gave a seat on the committee to the head of that firm. It was over for me.

There was also an entire generation of ambitious, impossible to manage young Turks coming up behind me, people who played the political game better than I did, twenty-somethings and thirty-somethings who didn't have small children who needed their parents home for supper. The young Turks could work late into the evening, billing the agency's clients for their after-hours time.

"I love those kids," the agency's CFO told me on the way to

the elevator at a quarter to six one evening, the place still full of hustling young creative people. "They never stop billing."

The same man, a member of the executive committee, once told me I couldn't possibly bill enough hours to pay for myself. Something was terribly wrong with my once meteoric career. I was suddenly postzenith. Ambivalence from above and ambition from below were combining to generate a subtle but insistent force that was propelling me toward the door, shouldering me down the old sow of an agency and pushing me lower and lower, from teat to teat. In no time at all, I was grubbing hard, barely holding on to that fabled hind one.

To understand where all this is going, you have to understand where real creativity comes from. It seeps from a festering pustule of insecurity deep in your soul's crotch. If you are a really creative person, you reach down there and squeeze it a little every day. You are flawed, and your flaw is the wellspring of your insecurity, and your insecurity is the wellspring of your creativity. So you squeeze. And you worry. If you sense yourself feeling confident, you tear it wide open. You continue to pick and worry away at it until your insecurity oozes the real stuff once more.

Advertising creativity is not a happy gift, and agency executives understand this. They foster your creativity by fostering your insecurity. They let you stew in your own juices. They leave you twisting in the wind. They incubate your idiosyncrasies. They sponsor award shows and fete the winners with trophies and honors.

When you are young and ambitious, you look forward to the shows. Later, the mere thought of them makes you start to melt and go whiney—as whiney as a four-year-old who has stayed too long at the mall. You come to realize the award shows exist not to honor the winners but to put the spur to the losers. You are under the gun to win something. You are a creative Sisyphus. You walk in the door the morning after, put your trophies on the shelf, turn around and find the creative rock is back at the bottom of the hill—hence the eighteen-hour days and the fitful six-hour nights, the alcoholism, the drugs, the divorces, and the children of your divorce in kiddy treatment for drug and alcohol problems and oozing fissures of angst of their own.

No real advertising creative is happy until he or she is miserable, and being miserable is addictive. There are copywriters who can't begin a day's work until they've spent an hour venting to their art director partner. They hate the agency that's paying them six figures. They hate the client who's paying the agency. They hate the new furniture in the lobby, the way the acounting department secretary dresses, the toilet paper in the bathroom. They hate, they hate, they hate. Somehow, hate gets the old creative pustule seeping.

There I was, VP, ACD, career in the tank, miserable, hating everything and everyone, juices flowing. All revved up and no place to go. I was in creative no-man's-land. A rung or two lower on the ladder, I might have tapped into my inner misery and created some truly great advertising. But I was VP, ACD now. I didn't create ads any more. I presented the young Turks' work to the client and sold my ass off to make the client buy it. If I couldn't sell their stuff, the young Turks saw me as a punched-out, skanked-up client whore. And most of their work was just plain unsalable. There was silly, frivolous, creatively masturbatory stuff intended to wow awards show judges, stuff that emulated some other agency's stuff, and stuff warmed over from last season's award show books, hence really not very creative at all. It was like trying to sell a red plaid sport coat to a customer who walked in wearing a dark blue suit. The harder I sold, the more the clients resented my persistence.

So while the executive committee met to vote themselves bonuses and plot the agency's future, I was down the hall, smothering the young Turks' second-rate ideas, calling their babies ugly, pleading with them to go back and try once more for something that better reflected the marketing strategy—something salable.

I wanted them to produce what poor, twisted Ezra Pound called "the fogged language of the swindling classes." I encouraged them to fog all the language they could in the service of the agency's swindling classes. But down deep, I didn't believe in advertising anymore. I saw now it was a trick. It was just being clever.

Besides, the swindling classes were swindling me. I couldn't advance in the organization. There was nowhere to go but away, and I had three small children. I couldn't afford to go away.

There was one other option. I had to try to be more valuable to the company. If I could find something to do that no one else would do, I might be able to regain control of the bobsled ride to hell that my career had become, which is why I volunteered to fog language on the ammunition account.

There are certain moneymaking accounts that advertising young Turks don't want to work on. These include dull, detail-intensive accounts that don't offer chic creative opportunities and morally questionable accounts that drop vast quantities of cash to the bottom line in a hurry. Tobacco accounts are like that, so are liquor accounts and farm chemicals. The ammunition account was that sort of business—riddled with details from calibers to muzzle velocities, long on bad karma (there was that killing thing), and short on award show opportunities. The account called for a pro's pro. I had qualms, plenty of them, but if no one else wanted to write the stuff (and no one did), I would put my qualms aside, wade in, and sell the goddamned bullets. You bet. No problem. Can do.

You may start out writing ammunition advertising with the idea that it's all about target shooting and hunting. You may think you can bluff your way through with a photo of a black lab with a dead mallard in its mouth. Ten minutes with your new client will disabuse you of that misperception. The ammunition business is about selling bullets and shotgun shells to sportsmen, to law enforcement agencies, and to anyone else with a gun who needs to reload. The ammunition business is about designing and manufacturing the kind of bullets the customer wants, from big, slow shotgun slugs to jacketed hollow-point pistol ammunition and super-fast, super-precise rounds for sniper rifles. The ammunition business is full of good ol' boys, soldiers of fortune, NRA types, FBI wannabes, and buyers for chain stores and mass merchandisers.

At that time, the ammunition business was good. The Democrats were in the White House, and a Democrat in the White House always makes gun owners nervous. The gun owners were buying all the ammunition they could find and caching it up—burying it out in the woods in some cases—in case the Democrats tried to take away their guns.

The good times were rolling at the bullet factory. They were working three shifts a day. The swindling classes who owned company stock were getting record dividends. But advertising professional or not, I just couldn't get over the hump and get with the program. I would tour the factory, walk through the warehouse, look at all those cases of bullets and shotgun shells, and wonder how many dead people they would make. How many paraplegics?

I could sense the karmic crosshairs centered on a target in the middle of my back. I could feel the bad juju piling up. I'd advertised fourteen-mile-a-gallon Ford LTDs during an oil embargo. I'd advertised usurious personal loans for a finance company. Now I was writing on the bullet account. What to do?

I did what any good adman does. I contrived a new set of morals for myself. I contorted logic in order to get out ahead of my sins. I volunteered at church and did some pro bono work for my kids' school. I dabbled in Buddhism a bit (whenever things get stressful, I dabble in Buddhism). But you can't really have morals in advertising. You can't keep fogging language for the swindling classes and expect to pay off your karmic debt any more than a billionaire can expect to buy his way into heaven.

I couldn't sleep. I was drinking too much. I was full of self-loathing, and why shouldn't I have been? I was compromising my ethics to make money for the executive committee so that they might vote themselves bonuses and send a big check to London where another executive committee would wet their beaks and distribute the rest to stockholders. It was one big karmic daisy chain in which I was somehow screwing myself.

The day finally came when I couldn't take it anymore. I walked into the president/creative director's office and quit. Two weeks to the day later, they threw a lunch for me, gave me a fancy fountain pen and some stationery, and shook my hand in the elevator lobby.

It has been fifteen years now. I wish I could say I'd sworn off advertising, but there are kids to feed and a mortgage to pay. I'm still out there, fogging language—just not on the bullet account. I feel better about that, I guess. But sometimes, late at night when I can't sleep, I sit in the Barcalounger and stare out the bedroom window. I look up into the starry night sky and contemplate the huge karma turd hurtling toward me.

A Bedside Visit

The last time I saw my father, he was lying in the bed nearest the door of a double-occupancy nursing-home room. Beside him, on one of those tables that wheel across the bed at mealtime, he had a glass of water with a flexible straw. A covered plastic pitcher of ice water gone tepid stood beside the glass. He had his glasses on, although he'd lost most of his ability to read by then. He was staring at the wall beyond the foot of the bed, killing what little time he had left.

He had aspirated his false teeth during a recent cardiovascular episode, and the nursing staff had retrieved the teeth and confiscated them. Almost defiantly, he'd taken to sticking a toothpick in the corner of his mouth and keeping it there all day. He would pull it out, hold it between his thumb and forefinger, and gesture with it—a miniature scepter—to add weight or inflection to his words.

One night, when my sister was there, he pulled the toothpick out. "That's Jerry," he said in that far-off voice the soon-to-be-dead acquire. He jerked the toothpick in the direction of his moaning, comatose roommate. "He doesn't put his toys away when he's done playing with them."

My sister glanced over her shoulder at Jerry. Absent bedclothes, hospital gown riding up, he was clutching at himself from somewhere deep in his coma—somewhere the other side of his own series of strokes, heart attacks, and other episodes.

175

That had been weeks earlier. My father was talking less now. Receding. Every episode took more of his spark and will and energy.

I'd left a business meeting in Pennsylvania and flown to Chicago to see him. Home was Minnesota, where my wife was pregnant and due any day. I was planning on spending the night at a brother's house, seeing my father the next day, then heading north. It was almost eight when I arrived at my brother's. Half an hour later, he, his wife, and I were sitting around the dining room table, talking, when the phone rang. It was my father.

"Come see me," he said, the words slurred and distant.

"It's too late, John," I told him. "Visiting hours are over. It'll be ten before I can get there. I'll see you tomorrow."

"I might not be here tomorrow."

So there he was, staring at the wall, toothpick protruding, on that plastic-covered mattress, in that terrible nighttime hospital lighting. The hallway was dark, the nursing station just outside the door quiet. In the semidarkness off to my right, Jerry glubbed and groaned.

My father and I had spent time together like this before, up in Wisconsin at the hospital near their place on the lake the day after his second big stroke, the one that had really launched this downhill run. He'd gotten up from the supper table, gone to his favorite chair, and tried to light a cigar—one of the four or five cheap cigars he smoked every day after the first stroke, when he'd quit smoking cigarettes. He hadn't been able to align the flame and the tip of the cigar. The flame was a good three inches off to the right. Then his speech had begun to thicken. My mother and I had put him in the car and driven eight miles through the fall twilight to the hospital emergency room. It was a beautiful evening. The last of the sunlight bounced off the undersides of a patch of feathery clouds.

"That's a mackerel sky," my father had slurred from the backseat, testing the wiring between his brain and his tongue, gauging the stroke's progress. "Tha-uh-ma-er-uhl ky."

We spent several hours in the emergency room, then they admitted him, and my mother and I returned to the lake for the night. She visited him early the next morning. I came to town and spelled her through the middle of the day.

His speech came back slightly, but it wasn't good. He spoke with that rubber-lipped, aphasic slur. He pointed to the "No Smoking, Oxygen in Use" sign on the wall across from his bed and said he was thinking hard about the message. No more smoking anything if he got out of there. There wasn't much more to talk about. We lapsed into silence. The afternoon crawled by.

Fifteen months later, there I was, sitting beside his bed in one of those not-quite-comfortable hospital easy chairs, listening to Jerry glug and bubble. My father stared down the bed at the wall while I fumbled, cross-tabbed, and searched for something to talk about. My wife, our kids, family life in Minnesota, my job—nothing seemed appropriate. Nothing bridged the two-and-a-half-foot void.

He was resigned to death by then, but a week earlier, he'd wanted my older brother to help him escape.

"Get the car," he said as my brother pushed him down the hall in a wheelchair. "Push me to the front entrance, go get the car, and we'll get out of here."

"No can do, John," my brother said. "You're too sick."

"I'm serious," my father had said. "Go get the car. Let's go."

"Sorry. Too sick."

My father thought about it as my brother rolled him down the hall. After a minute, he said, "You mean to tell me a couple of smart guys like us can't think our way out of here?"

He'd come to accept it now. There was no thinking his way out of this. There were only loose ends to wrap up, and there didn't seem to be words to wrap them up with. The family had always seemed cool and standoffish. With eleven of us and a bath and a half, there hadn't been a lot of room in which to be demonstrative, so we rarely said "I love you." Not in so many words. My father's father had been an alcoholic, and my father had had his emotions shoved back in his face too many times when he was growing up. Then there was his own alcoholism—that and World War II and forty years covering Chicago as a news reporter had convinced him the best thing he could do for his children was raise us tough.

Tough meant never being surprised by what the world threw at you. Tough meant being thick-skinned and rolling with the punch. So we rarely heard "I love you" from him. The best he could do was shake your hand at bedtime and mutter, "We got love, hunh," almost under his breath, off to the side, where no one could get any leverage on it and shove it back in his face.

Sitting in that room with him was like waiting with someone at the bus station, the two of you sitting around, waiting for the PA system to call "all aboard."

Once, helping him fix the lawnmower when I was twelve, I accidentally kicked over a coffee can full of gas and lawnmower parts he'd been cleaning. Things had gone every which way. The gas had seeped down through the gravel driveway into the dirt.

"God damn you," he said.

He'd said it reflexively, not deliberately, but he had said it, and he never said he was sorry or taken it back. He wasn't a man for apologies. He didn't operate that way.

"I never laid a hand on my kids," an advertising friend of mine told me over his second Manhattan at lunch one day. "But I damn sure abused them."

I knew what the man meant.

After his first stroke, when he was considering retirement, I wrote my father a long letter urging him not to do it. He should keep working and stay involved in the world. He didn't respond. Weeks went by, then months. I finally happened through Chicago on business and dropped by his office to say hello. The stroke had gimped up his left side, but he stumped downstairs to the company cafeteria and bought coffee for us, and we sat there, short on conversation yet again. I asked if he got the letter. He had. I asked what he thought.

"I think you don't know what you're talking about," he said.

If I hadn't known what I was talking about in that letter, I sure didn't know what I was talking about there in the dark nursing home. I had nothing. Afraid he would shove it back in my face, I sat there stymied, and when he finally fell asleep, I got up and went back to my brother's house.

I caught an early flight back to Minnesota the next morning. My wife and I had a big, beautiful baby boy the following week. My father died the week after that—on Valentine's Day.

Vigil Candles

I had a dream before dawn this morning. One of those camera-subjective things where the dream wandered, boomed, pushed, and panned around and through the vigil lights on Saint Joseph's side of the altar in an old Catholic church. Some of the candles were newly lit; others were old, weakly flaming, on the verge of flickering out; others were at various stages in between. Still others had yet to be lit at all. Every so often a coin would clank into a brass collection box outside the camera frame and echo in the empty church. Then some hand, holding a twisted, waxed-paper wick, would reach into the shot, borrow flame from one of the candles, and light a new one.

Even asleep, the allegory was obvious. The candles were people. The flames were lives. I'm not sure whose hand it was, but the dream wandered through time—something I've been doing more and more myself lately.

All my dearly and not so dearly departed were there—some long extinguished, others more recently, interspersed with living, young and old, and with generations yet to come. And I don't think it was an accident that this was Saint Joseph's side of the altar. The man married into chaos. He was an in-law, immersed in the story up to here. But let's face it, he was not real family, and somewhere down deep, we all count ourselves in-laws, not real family, to the rest of humanity.

180

It was a substantial dream, and it stayed long enough for me to fix it in my memory after I woke up. I've been working away at it all day today, picking and poking, putting it aside and letting it fester, then coming back to it, thinking about people I've known and people yet to come. It seems to want to run parallel to a certain way I've come to see the world as I walk through it.

I live in Minneapolis. The city was here one hundred and twenty years before I showed up, and it's full of old tenements and warehouses and bridges and schools, lakes and parks, defunct corner grocery stores, and house, duplex, and small-apartment neighborhoods. It feels beautifully haunted to me. I walk through it and sense other generations looking out from the city's windows. I feel other times.

There's a stone-arch railroad bridge dating back to the late 1800s—a walking and biking path across the Mississippi now. The bridge curves across the flow of the river just below Saint Anthony Falls. Halfway across, out in the middle, there's a spot where I sit and sense all the passengers, trains, and years. I got my first view of the city from a railroad-car window right about where I like to sit now.

A couple miles to the south, on the west bank of the river in a neighborhood off Franklin Avenue, is an old duplex where I overstayed my welcome with friends one summer, freeloading, waiting for the army to send me to Vietnam and my world to implode. A few miles west is a bus bench on a Bloomington Avenue corner that will forever be special to me.

I have venues like this all over the city—old, but still callow places. I look up at certain windows and know the rooms on the other side of the glass. I see the chandeliers with flame-shaped bulbs still hanging over the place where the dining room table goes years after I last walked out. I remember people who no longer live there and things that happened there—winter-evening card games, holiday parties, loves and friendships abandoned.

So much unfinished business—so much dust in this or that corner of the city, in this or that corner of time. So many snapshots stored in a shoebox way at the back of the bedroom closet shelf.

Am I being too loyal to old friends and lovers? To my old self? To events that don't mean anything to anyone anymore? We each have an irretrievable past, right over there on the other side of everything that has happened since. We each had a hand in letting large and small things go, and we can't ever again put it together the way it was. Who the hell would want to? But here I am, stupid old bastard, wandering the city, missing people and events, feeling sorry for myself.

I seem to be serving a life sentence on a committee of one, futilely planning a big reunion to which no one will come, not even me.

Biking past the duplex where I overstayed my welcome a while ago, I sensed myself, young, sitting on the front steps, smoking, killing time. For a second there, I really was my young self again. It was all I could do not to look up and watch my present self bicycle away. Sometimes on the bridge I all but glimpse my younger self looking out at the city from that railroad-car window.

I owe five dollars to a man I'll never see again—a college friend who opened his wallet and handed the money to me one day when I was broke. I hadn't asked for it. He just gave me the money and told me to pay him when I could. He left school two weeks later. I never saw him again. There was that beautiful young woman at that beach on the South China Sea in Vietnam. She was swimming. She waved for me to come out and join her. There was the granddaughter of a Russian duke I met while I was stationed in Germany. She sent me a postcard from Versailles. It arrived at mail call in the motor pool just as I was leaving with a convoy of trucks heading up Highway 1 to Nha Trang.

There was my mother's Aunt Flo, a widow who took care of my great-grandmother and gave us boxes of monogrammed handkerchiefs and Parker T-Ball Jotter pens and Salerno butter cookies at Christmas. There was my great-grandmother herself, past ninety, hard of hearing, looking a bit addled but speaking precise nineteenth-century English with the brogue she'd brought from County Limerick seventy-three years earlier.

All these people and places and a thousand-thousand more. Time works its way into cracks, expands, and pushes us apart, even away from ourselves.

A coin clanks. A hand reaches in, borrows a flame, lights another candle. And, for some reason, I find myself half-remembering a letter my father wrote in which he described the cheap shoes with curled toes on the old Irish parish priest's feet as he lay in his casket at his wake. My father didn't write about the priest's shoes maliciously, then again, he wasn't afraid to point to the humor in the small detail he'd noted.

Years later, after he'd been cremated, my mother had my father's ashes buried in a full-sized cemetery plot. She took me to see the grave a week or two later, and there was the scar where the gravedigger had opened a small square hole—only a spade's width by a spade's width—and planted my father. The entire process couldn't have taken more than two minutes. My father would have found his own grave funny—funnier than the priest's cheap shoes.

Peter Smith is a thirty-year veteran of Twin Cities advertising and a regular contributor to *Morning Edition* on Minnesota Public Radio. He writes magazine features, fiction, and occasional op-ed pieces. He is author of *A Porch Sofa Almanac* (Minnesota, 2010). He and his wife live in Hopkins, Minnesota.